Franklin Leonard Pope

The western Boundary of Massachusetts

A Study of Indian and colonial History

Franklin Leonard Pope

The western Boundary of Massachusetts
A Study of Indian and colonial History

ISBN/EAN: 9783337153984

Printed in Europe, USA, Canada, Australia, Japan

Cover: Foto ©ninafisch / pixelio.de

More available books at **www.hansebooks.com**

The Western

Boundary of Massachusetts.

FRANKLIN LEONARD POPE.

THE

WESTERN BOUNDARY

OF

MASSACHUSETTS:

A STUDY OF

INDIAN AND COLONIAL HISTORY.

BY

FRANKLIN LEONARD POPE.

MEMBER OF THE BERKSHIRE HISTORICAL AND SCIENTIFIC SOCIETY

PITTSFIELD, MASS
PRIVATELY PRINTED.
1886.

PREFACE.

In the following historical sketch, the substance of which was embodied in a paper read at the quarterly meeting of the Berkshire Historical and Scientific Society, in May, 1835, an attempt has been made to trace with some care the sequence of events which led to the final establishment of the existing boundary between the states of Massachusetts and New York. The history of this particular boundary has been involved in political complications, which tend to confer upon it a more than local and temporary consequence. Indeed, it is not improbable that the collateral results of the present investigation may be, by many, regarded as of more interest, if not actually of greater importance, than those more immediately aimed at. Among the indirect results which have thus rewarded the author's researches, may be mentioned the new light which has been thrown upon the local history of the Indian nation originally occupying the country between the Hudson and Connecticut Rivers; a connected relation of the origin, progress, and results of the anti-rent troubles, which disturbed the peace and good order of the state of New York for more than a century; and the important fact, now for the first time clearly established, that the permanent settlement of Berkshire county was commenced by pioneers from the valley of the Hudson, at a very much earlier date than has hitherto been supposed.

In the preparation of this paper, the unpublished manuscript archives of the states of Massachusetts, Connecticut and New York, as well as many county and town records, have been freely consulted and have yielded much valuable material. The present relation can be considered as scarcely more than an outline, and hence the authorities for all important statements made have been indicated, so far as practicable, for the convenience of future investigators. The author desires to express his grateful acknowledgments to the custodians of the several state, county and town archives, as well as to those friends who have aided in the collection of material and otherwise facilitated his labors.

EDGEWOOD FARM, *Elizabeth, N. J., June* 1, 1886.

THE WESTERN BOUNDARY OF MASSA-
CHUSETTS.

A STUDY OF INDIAN AND COLONIAL HISTORY.

The adjustment of the boundary lines between Massachu-setts Bay and the adjacent colonies and provinces, is a subject which for generations furnished a most prolific occasion of con-troversy and disagreement between the authorities and the in-habitants of the several governments concerned therein. The historian who has had no occasion to investigate the matter, can form but an inadequate conception of the vast volume of legislation, negotiation and correspondence relative to this sub-ject which encumber the dusty archives of the ancient colonial governments. It would have been well if this were all, but these same records afford abundant evidence that the boundary disputes originated, or at all events furnished a convenient pre-text for many angry altercations and riotous assemblages, which not infrequently—at least in the case of the particular bounda-ry to which this investigation relates—terminated in armed conflicts attended with no inconsiderable loss of life.

There is perhaps no reason to suppose that Massachusetts has sinned in this respect beyond any of her sister states, for it is a matter of history that to a greater or less extent the same causes of difference have existed elsewhere, and have necessarily pro-duced similar results. It has been truthfully observed that while adjacent landholders may take but little note of the title, quality or culture of their neighbor's fields, they are neverthe-less certain to evince a lively and abiding interest in the ques-tion of the proper location of the division fences. It is this in-stinctive jealousy, a feeling which is shared by every one of us in respect to the possible encroachments of neighbors upon his territorial possessions, which lends a certain degree of contem-poraneous human interest to the subject of this paper. In the case of the boundary between the provinces of Massachusetts

and New York, the bitterness of the controversy was intensified
by the presence of conditions which did not exist elsewhere.
It involved not only a conflict of different nationalities but of
antagonistic political institutions. To look upon this contention
merely as a trial of conclusions between the English and Dutch
settlers and their respective descendants would be to underesti-
mate its true significance, for it involved something far more important than this; it was nothing less than a death-struggle between the free land-tenures and independent town organizations
of the Massachusetts colony, and the antiquated feudal system
under which the adjacent territories of the province of New
York were held and governed. While the quarrel had its origin
in the selfish greed of individuals, yet from beginning to
end these peculiar political and social conditions exercised a
potent influence upon the character of the proceedings, and
confer upon the subject a degree of historical interest and importance which under other circumstances it might not have
possessed.

The original rights of sovereignty and dominion assumed in
America by the great European powers were founded in the
first instance upon the basis of prior discovery and possession :
rights into the origin of which it is not proposed to inquire, but
which are founded upon ancient and immemorial usage. Under
the law of nations, the mere fact of prior discovery constitutes
in itself but an imperfect or inchoate title, unless followed
by actual occupation, and a formal declaration of the intention of the sovereign or state to take possession. But it
should be understood that the titles asserted in the royal grants
were against other European nations only. The English, the
French and the Dutch, alike asserted an exclusive claim to the
sovereignty and jurisdiction of their respective discoveries, but
the right in the soil was in fact limited to the privilege of pre-
emption, or in other words, the exclusive right to purchase at
the owner's price such lands as the natives might be disposed
to sell, not the right to coerce from them an unwilling surrender of their territory. In accordance with this traditional
policy, each colonial government, within its own limits, asserted
and enforced an exclusive right to extinguish Indian titles by

fair purchase, under the sanction of treaties made by the natives collectively in open council. All private purchases, whether from the Indians individually, or collectively as tribes, were held to be absolutely null and void. Hence a governmental grant was the only source of territorial title of which the validity was admitted in the courts of justice.[1]

The authorities of the several colonies appear on the whole to have treated the Indians with praiseworthy justice and moderation. There were isolated instances, it is true, in which the lands of the Indians were wrongfully appropriated or the stipulated compensation withheld. Through corrupt political influences, or by misrepresentation and fraud, unscrupulous individuals sometimes succeeded in obtaining a *prima facie* title to lands to which they had no right, but cases of this kind may fairly have been said to be exceptional.[2]

The English claim to that portion of the continent of North America included in the great patent of James I. in 1606, was founded on the discoveries of Sebastian Cabot, who in 1497–8 sailed at a distance along the Atlantic coast between the fortieth and forty-eighth parallels of latitude.

The claim of the Dutch was founded upon the discoveries of Henry Hudson and Adrian Block. Hudson, an English mariner in the service of the Dutch West India Company, sailed from Holland in the spring of 1609, and after an adventurous voyage anchored within the mouth of the river afterwards called the Delaware. Thence coasting northward he entered the lower bay of New York, and in September 1609, after having spent a few days in the examination of the adjacent shores and waters he cautiously ascended the river called by the natives the Mahicanituk,[3] until on the seventeenth of that month he dropped anchor nearly opposite what is now Castleton. Here he landed,

---

1. Kent's Commentaries. (8th Ed.) III, 401–402.

2. As early as 1633, Massachusetts formally prohibited the purchase of land from the natives without license from the government, and Plymouth in 1643 passed a similar law. In New Netherlands a like honorable policy was pursued from the first by the Dutch, and afterward continued by their successors. Immediately after the conquest by the English in 1665, it was ordained that no purchase of lands from the Indians should be valid, without the license of the governor and the execution of the purchase in his presence.

3. According to Heckewelder, this was the name given to the river by the Delawares and other southern tribes, signifying literally, the place of the Mahicans. The Mahicans themselves called it the Shatemuc. The Iroquois name appears to have been Cahohatatea. Coll. N. Y. Hist. Soc. I, 43.

and, as it is related, upon invitation accompanied an Indian sachem to his wigwam where he was hospitably entertained.[1] After sending an exploring party in a boat at least as far as what is now Waterford, Hudson returned to the mouth of the Mahicanituk, and sailed homeward, reaching Dartmouth, England, on the seventh of November, from whence he forwarded an account of his discoveries to his employers. The next year a company of Amsterdam merchants dispatched a trading vessel to the newly discovered river, and in 1612 and 1613, a number of similar commercial ventures were undertaken. In the autumn of 1613, one of the Dutch vessels commanded by Adrian Block was accidentally burned just as she was about to sail from the river on her return voyage. In consequence of this misfortune, Block and his crew were obliged to winter among the natives, in huts which they erected on Manhattan island.[2] During the winter Block built a small yacht,[3] and in the spring undertook a voyage of exploration to the eastward. Sailing along the northern shore of the sound, he visited what he named the "River of Roodenberg," or Red Hills, which he described as "about a bow-shot wide." To Block therefore, must be ascribed the honor of the first discovery of our own beautiful river, the Housatonic. Still further eastward he came to the mouth of a large river—the Connecticut—which he named the Fresh river. He ascended this as far as the foot of the rapids near the present village of Windsor Locks, where he found a fortified Indian village. Returning thence to the sound, he successively visited the localities now known as Thames river, Montauk Point, Block Island, Narragansett Bay, the Vineyard, Nantucket, and Nahant.[4] Six years therefore before the Pilgrims landed at Plymouth, all the prominent localities on the southern and southeastern coast of New England had been vis-

1. A detailed account of Hudson's exploration of the river and bay, derived from Juet's journal of Hudson's third voyage, and De Laet's narrative, is given in Brodhead's History of New York, i. 26-34. See also Yates &. Moulton's History of New York, i. 261-272.

2. Brodhead's Hist. New York, i. 48.

3. This was the first vessel built in New Netherland, and was named the *Onrust* (Restless.) It was forty-four and a half feet long, eleven and a half feet beam, and of about 8 lasts, or 16 tons burden. Col. History of New York, i. 13; Brodhead's New York, i 53.

4. Brodhead's Hist. New York, i. 55-56.

ited and examined by this enterprising Dutch explorer. From
Cape Cod, he returned to Holland, and in the following year
supervised the preparation of a map embodying his discoveries.[1]
Armed with this map as an exhibit, the Amsterdam merchants
now petitioned the States-General of the Netherlands for a trading charter to the regions which had been made known by the
enterprise of the Dutch navigators. The request was at once
complied with, and on the 10th of October, 1614, the charter
of the "Directors of New Netherlands" was passed and duly
sealed, granting them the exclusive right "to visit and navigate
to the aforesaid newly discovered lands lying in America, between New France and Virginia, the sea coasts whereof extend
from the fortieth to the forty-fifth degree of latitude, now
named New Netherland, (as is to be seen on the Figurative Map
prepared by them,) for four voyages within the period of three
years, commencing on the first day of January, 1615, next en-
suing, or sooner."[2]

In 1614 a fortified trading post called Fort Nassau was established near what is now Albany, and Jacob Eelkins, its com-
mandant, ere long succeeded in establishing a lucrative traffic in
furs, while he kept scouting parties constantly engaged in exploring the surrounding wilderness and in cultivating friendly
relations with the native inhabitants.[3]

A mutually advantageous treaty of peace and friendship was
concluded at an early day between the whites and the Indians
at Fort Nassau, which remained unbroken for more than one
hundred and fifty years.[4]

The first English exploration of the southern coast of New England took place in 1619, in which year Captain Thomas Dermer,
sailing from Monhegan near the Kennebec, rounded Cape Cod,
passed inside of Long Island, and thence to James river. The
following year he returned, making a more careful examination
of the shores,[5] after which he transmitted his report to his em-

1. The original of this map, which is beautifully executed on parchment, is in the archives at the Hague. It is the most ancient map extant of the coast of southern New England and New York. A fac simile is in the office of the Secretary of State at Albany. A detailed description of it may be found in Brodhead's Hist. New York, I. 755-6.
2. New York Col. Hist., I. 10.
3. Brodhead's Hist. New York, I. 55, 67, 755.
4. Doc. Hist. New York, III. 51; Brodhead's Hist. New York, I. 81.
5. Dermer's letter Dec. 27, 1619, in New York Hist. Soc. Coll., I. 352.

ployer, Sir Fernando Gorges,[1] who with thirty associates constituting the Plymouth company, had already petitioned the king for a charter. The information communicated by Derner no doubt spurred them in their efforts, and at length they were fortunate enough to receive the royal assent to their petition.[2]

The great patent of New England, thus granted by James the First in 1620, to "the Council established at Plymouth in the county of Devon for the planting, ruling and governing of New England in America," granted to that corporation all that part of the continent of North America lying between the fortieth and forty-eighth degrees of north latitude "throughout the main land from sea to sea, provided the same or any part be not actually possessed or inhabited by any other Christian prince or state," together with a complete monopoly of its trade and absolute powers of legislation and government.[3] The subsequent grants of the soil of the several New England colonies were issued under this patent.

Meanwhile the charter of the Amsterdam mercantile adventurers had expired by limitation, and their enterprise was succeeded by a great commercial organization, chartered by the States General of the United Netherlands in 1621, as the West India Company, with the most ample power to colonize, govern and defend the territories of New Netherland.[4] Under the auspices of this company permanent colonization was commenced in 1623, in which year Fort Orange was erected on the present site of Albany,[5] and Fort Nassau on the South or Delaware river. Two families were also sent to the Fresh or Connecticut river, and a fort or trading post named Good Hope was commenced where Hartford now is. In 1626 Manhattan Island was purchased of the natives and a fortified settlement commenced, which soon became the commercial emporium of the new colony. It must therefore be admitted as an indisputable historical fact that the Dutch were the prior occupants as well as the prior discoverers of the country adjacent to the navigable portions of the Hudson, the Housatonic, the Connecticut and the Delaware.

1. Gorges' Brief Narration. Massachusetts Hist. Soc. Coll., xxvi. 61.
2. Order in Council, July 23, 1620. New York Col. Hist., III. 8.
3. Hazard's State Papers, I. 103-118; Trumbull's Connecticut, I. 510.
4. See charter at length. Hazard I. 121; O'Callaghan's New Netherland, I. 399.
5. Brodhead Hist. New York, III. 20, 50, 51.

The contradictory statements and opinions of historians concerning the tribal relations and geographical distribution of the aboriginal inhabitants of the valley of the Hudson and the mountainous region between that river and the Connecticut, have perhaps rather tended to increase than to dispel the obscurity which envelops the subject. It is certain that the early explorers and settlers found but comparatively few Indian families permanently occupying the upper Housatonic valley. Hence it was conjectured by Dr. Field, one of the earliest local chroniclers, that the defeat of the eastern tribes by the New England colonists during Philip's war in 1675; the precipitate flight of the remnant across the western mountains closely pursued by Major Talcott and the Connecticut troops, and the sanguinary encounter of the colonial forces with the fugitives at the ford-way of the Housatonic, "midway between Westfield and Fort Orange," caused many of the original native inhabitants to abandon their homes in alarm, and to flee to the westward, where they became incorporated with other tribes.[1] Gallatin says that "while the Pequots and Mohegans claimed some authority over the Indians of the Connecticut, those extending westwardly to the Hudson appear to have been divided into small and independent tribes, united, since they were known to the Europeans, by no common government." Smith, the historian of Pittsfield, while admitting what is unquestionably true, that at the date of the discovery, the nation known by the Dutch as the Mahicans, and by the English as the Mohegans, occupied the territory now comprised in the counties of Berkshire, Columbia and Rensselaer, goes on to state that the formation of the celebrated league of the Iroquois compelled the Mahicans to form an alliance with the Wappingers and other river tribes "with whom they had up to that time been at continual war," but that the allies were nevertheless vanquished by the Mohawks in a decisive battle fought near Rhinebeck not long before the advent of the whites, and the defeated party "reduced to vassalage." "In 1625," continues Smith, "the Mohicans attempted to regain their independence, but after a merciless war of three years duration, the greater portion of them were killed

1. History of Berkshire County, 14, 15.

or captured, and the remainder driven into the valley of the Connecticut, where they became incorporated with the Pequots."[1]   Again, the same author states that "the Iroquois, who had become the feudal lords of the old Mohegan empire, granted a refuge to a band of exiled Narragansetts, which grew to be the Scaghticoke tribe, and sent out little colonies to the valley of the Housatonic."[2]

It seems probable that Smith has been led into error by accepting without sufficient examination the incorrect assertions of O'Callaghan,[3] Brodhead[4] and other New York authorities. The Mohawks were for generations the petted adherents of the New York colonial government, and no opportunity has been neglected to enlarge upon their prowess. Almost every writer of colonial and Indian history has apparently taken for granted as an undisputed fact, the original supremacy of the Iroquois confederacy over all the neighboring nations. It is true that we find in the colonial annals comparatively few references to the history of the Mahican nation, but the true reason for this omission is not difficult to conjecture. Soon after the conquest of New Netherlands in 1664, when the trading post of Fort Orange came under the dominion of the English and received its new name of Albany, the Mahicans, originally the sole proprietors of the adjacent territory, for reasons which will hereafter be considered, withdrew to the eastward and became essentially a New England tribe, and thenceforth their affairs became, so far as the New York government was concerned, of secondary importance compared with those of the Mohawks and the confederate tribes to the westward. Establishing their headquarters in a remote and at that time almost utterly unexplored portion of Massachusetts, it is not surprising that so little can be found in the archives of that government respecting the Mahicans prior to the execution of the treaty at Westfield in 1724. In view of the facts disclosed by the colonial records, to some of which reference will presently be made, it may well be doubted if there is any foundation for the assertion that the Mahicans

1. Smith's History of Pittsfield, Mass., I, 48, 49, 50.
2. Ibid I, 47.
3. O'Callaghan's New Netherland, I, 850.
4. Brodhead's New York, I, 85, 87.

were at any period of their history "subjugated" or "reduced to vassalage" by the Mohawks, or that they were expelled from the valley of the Hudson as the result of an unsuccessful rebellion against their alleged oppressors.

At the date of the discovery, the Mahicans occupied both banks of the Hudson, their territories on the west side extending from the vicinity of Catskill as far north as the Mohawk river,[1] and westward to the foot of the Helderbergh mountains. This is proved by the indisputable evidence of Indian deeds in the New York archives. Van Rensselaer, the patroon, purchased of the Mahican owners in 1680, all their remaining land on the west side of the river, extending from Beeren Island[3] northward to the Mohawk river, and "in breadth two days' journey," a tract which constitutes the present county of Albany.[4] The site of Beaverwyck, now the city of Albany, had been purchased from the same tribe before the building of Fort Orange.[5] A number of Mahican families occupied a castle at Cohoes as late as 1660. It is apparent that the possession of both shores of a great river like the Hudson was an advantage no less important to these savages than it now is to their civilized successors. Its inexhaustible stores of fish furnished them with a certain means of subsistence at all seasons, and the navigation which it afforded greatly facilitated intercommunication and trade. If, therefore, the Mahicans had been vanquished, driven away and almost exterminated by the Mohawks in 1628, as asserted by the historian referred to, it is inconceivable that they could have been permitted to hold undisputed possession of the western shore until so late a date as 1680.[6]

The territory of the Mahican nation proper, at the date of the discovery, extended, as already stated, westward, two days' journey beyond the Hudson river, and northward along the

1. Wassenaer's History Von Europa, Amsterdam, 1621, says that the Mahicans held seventy-five English miles on both sides of the river above, and that the Maquas or Mohawks resided in the interior.—Doc. Hist. New York, III, 27, 28.

2. Ruttenber's Indian Tribes of Hudson's River, 34, 35; O'Callaghan's New Netherland, I, 123-24.

3. Literally Bear's Island, so called, no doubt from the totem of its occupants.

4. New York Records.

5. Ruttenber's Indian Tribes of Hudson's River, 58; New York Col. Hist., I, 512.

6. Deeds on record in the New York archives show that Aepjin, king of the Mahicans, kept his council fire at Schodack as late as 1664. Ruttenber, 58.

same river and the east side of Wood creek[1] and Lake Champlain as far as Otter creek in Vermont.[2] It was bounded on the east by the head waters of the Westfield and the main stream of the Tunxis or Farmington river,[3] and on the south by Rœliff Jansen's kill, a tributary of the Hudson, and probably also by Salmon creek, which flows from the westward into the Housatonic near Lime Rock station in Connecticut.[4] The ancient council-fire or seat of government was at Schodack, or Eskwatak, at which place their chief was visited by Hudson in 1609, as already mentioned.[5]

The Mahicans constituted one of several allied nations of common Algonquin descent,[6] speaking a language generically the same, whose territories extended over New England from Quebec to Manhattan. The confederacy also embraced the Lenni-Lenapes or Delawares, occupying the region watered by the western tributaries of the Hudson, below Catskill, as well as the extensive area east of the Alleghanies drained by the Delaware, the Susquehanna and the Potomac.[6]

That the Mahicans and Mohawks were hereditary enemies is indisputable, and that they were frequently at war with each other during the period of the Dutch dominion the records afford abundant evidence. In the last war with the Mohawks in

---

1. In the Mss. of Sir William Johnson in the N. Y. State Library (vol. xxi, 40) is a letter endorsed :—"Letter from Ohio concerning land—rec'd it Oct. 16th, 1771." This letter was from a Mahican Indian, Abraham, who had left his lands on Wood creek in 1730, and allied himself with the Delawares. In this letter he says :—" I understand the Mohikans at Stockbridge are wanting to sell a certain tract of land lying above Albany, from the mouth of Wood creek upwards." He claimed to still own the land, and protested against the sale. He says further, "It may be reported that I am dead, as it is forty years since I left that country." Signed, "Mohekin Abraham or Keependo."

2. See post. p. 40.

3. Captain Konkapot, at a conference with the settling committee of the Housatonic proprietary in February, 1730, said :—"All the land east of what I have sold to the committee, as far as Farmington river, and south to the Connecticut line is all my land." Taylor's Hist. Great Barrington, 64.

4. Deed of Mahican Indians to Robert Livingston, Doc. Hist. N. Y., III, 612; Ruttenber's Indian Tribes of Hudson's River, 83, 85.

5. This castle was located upon the site of the present village of Castleton, N. Y. The name Schodack is derived from the Algonquin *skootay*, fire, and *ak*, place.

6. President Edwards, who was a missionary among them at Stockbridge for several years, gives the name as Mohekaneuw, which as interpreted by themselves, signifies "the people of the great waters continually in motion," in allusion to the ancestral tradition of the nation that they originally emigrated from the north-western coast of North America. President Dwight writes the name Muhhekanneuw. (Dwight's Travels, II, 365.) They were called Mahikanders by the Dutch, and Mourigans and Mauliniganns by the French. The English orthography of the records is, as usual, various. Mahikans, Mohicons, Mohegans, are some of the more common forms. For a list of twenty-six variants of the name see N. Y. Colonial Hist., gen. index, p. 303. The traditional history of the nation is given in detail in Mass. Hist. Coll., ix, 101. An interesting account of the national customs, etc., is in Jones' Stockbridge, Past and Present.

6. Ruttenber's Indian Tribes of Hudson's River, 45.

1664 we learn that the Mahican nation and its eastern allies assembled in great numbers at a place nine miles east of Claverack, probably at or near the outlet of Ach-kook-peeck or Copake lake, and soon after made a furious descent upon the Mohawks, defeating them with great slaughter.[1] This war continued with varying fortunes for two or three years, the balance of
success inclining decidedly in favor of the Mahicans, until peace
was finally restored through the influence of the authorities of
New York and Massachusetts.[2]

At a date not precisely known, but probably between 1680
and 1690, the capital of the Mahican nation appears to have
been removed from Eskwatak to the Housatonic[3] valley. The
reason assigned for the removal has usually been that the Mahicans were driven from their ancient haunts by their implacable
enemies, the Mohawks.[4] There appears to be no evidence
whatever that this was actually the case. A far more probable
and reasonable explanation is to be looked for in the fact that
the Mahicans had sold all their territories in the Hudson valley,
with a few unimportant exceptions, to the colonists.[5] The patents of Rensselaerwyck, Kinderhook, Patkook and Livingston,
all of which had been disposed of before 1685, embraced almost
the entire territory along the east shore of the Hudson extending from Roeloff Jansen's kill to the Hoosick river. It is altogether probable therefore, that having thus parted with their
lands, they peaceably retired further into the wilderness, and it

---

1. Doc. Hist. New York, iv. 84, 85.

2. Letter of Gov. Lovelace to Gov. Winthrop in 1669, vide Ruttenber's Indian Tribes of Hudson's River, p. 100 (note.)

3. The derivation of the name Housatonic has given rise to a great deal of discussion. The terminal syllable (Alg. *uk*, "place") shows that the name did not belong originally to the river, but to the valley. Dr. Dwight, on the authority of President Edwards, gives the name as Hoo-es-ten-nue, and the signification as "over the mountain." Dwight's Travels, I. 8.) According to Trumbull, this interpretation is sustained by analysis: *wussi* (Delaware, *awussi*; Chippewa, *wassa*, *wans'uch*; Abnaki, *awus* or *aoas*), meaning "beyond," "on the other side of;" *adene*, "mountain," and *uk*, "place" or "land." Eunice Mahwee, the last full-blood survivor of the Scaticoke band of Kent, Conn., in 1858, pronounced the name *Hous'-a-ten-uc*, and also interpreted it "over the mountain." (Moravian Memorial, p. 75. Trumbull's Indian names in Conn.) Rev. J. Slingerland, of Kesehem, Wis., a Stockbridge Indian of pure blood, pronounces the name *Ou-thol-ton-nook*, the first syllable having the sound of ou as in out, and gives the same definition. (Taylor's Hist. Great Barrington, 12, 13.) These concurrent authorities establish the proper interpretation of the name beyond reasonable doubt, although fanciful attempts have been made to show that the original form of the word was Dutch, Westenook, meaning "west corner." Smith's Hist. Pittsfield. I. 16–21. But there is no apparent reason why the Dutch should have given the appellation "west corner" to a tract of land on their extreme eastern frontier, and hence this explanation, although supported by a chain of ingenious and plausible conjecture, can scarcely be admitted.

4. Page 85 ante.

5. Page 87 ante, (notes 1 and 2.)

may be conjectured that they re-established their council-fire at Wah-nah-ti-kook in the present town of Stockbridge. That this place was in fact the capital of the Mahican nation at the time of the first settlement of the English on the Housatonic would seem to admit of little doubt.

Loskiel, the Moravian,—a most excellent authority on all matters concerning the Indians—writing from Gnadenhutten, in Pennsylvania in 1751, says:—"Two deputies were likewise sent to the great council of the Mahican nation at Westenhuck, with which they appeared much pleased, and as a proof of their satisfaction made Abraham, an assistant at Gnadenhutten, a captain."[1]   President Dwight, writing of the Stockbridge Indians in 1793, says:—"This tribe was, both by itself and other tribes, acknowledged to be the *eldest branch* of their nation; and as such regularly had precedence in their councils.[2]   Dr. Field states that "although their number was now small, they belonged to a large tribe of Indians who had been commonly called by the English *River Indians*, some of whom lived in the northwest corner of Connecticut, and more at various places westward within the bounds of New York."[3]

Even more conclusive is the evidence contained in a treaty executed at the great council at Fort Stanwix in 1768, between the Mohawks and the Stockbridge Indians, in which these nations agreed that the "just and true" boundary between their respective possessions was the Hudson river as far up as Fort Edward, and thence along Wood creek and Lake Champlain to the northward, and mutually released all pretensions which each may have had to lands on the opposite side of this boundary.[4]

1. Hist. Moravian Missions. Part III. p. 140.
2. Dwight's Travels. II. 387.
3. Hist. of Berkshire Co., 240.
4. In September 1768, pursuant to instructions from the Crown, a large number of Indians, comprising delegates from the Six Nations, Shawnees, Delawares, Senecas, and Mahicans, assembled at Fort Stanwix, the present site of Rome, N. Y., for the purpose of entering into a treaty with the Commissioners of Pennsylvania, New Jersey and Virginia, and Sir William Johnson, Superintendent of Indian affairs, to settle a boundary line between the Colonies and the Indians. A report of the proceedings at this treaty, in the form of a journal, is in New York Col. Hist. viii. 111–137. In this occurs the following entry:—"30th [September.] The Bounds between the Mohawks and the Stockbridge Indians were adjusted to mutual satisfaction and the latter returned home." In 1884, the author by accident discovered in the Connecticut State archives at Hartford, a Ms. copy of the agreement referred to, the only one known to be in existence. It is in Indians, II. 525. A copy of this interesting document is printed in the appendix. The signers in behalf of the Stockbridge nation are Jacob Naunnaumphtaunu, John Konkapot and Solomon Uhhannaumwaunut, three of the principal sachems.

The Mahicans, therefore, were no unworthy occupants of the beautiful region which constituted their ancient possessions. From first to last they resolutely maintained their independence, and on all occasions seem to have proved themselves fully a match for the confederated warriors of the west.

The subsequent history of the Mahican or Stockbridge nation has been written by abler pens than mine, and I need not therefore dwell upon it. The inscription upon the monument which pious and reverent hands have reared above their dust in the old Indian burial ground at Stockbridge:—"The ancient burial place of the Stockbridge Indians, the friends of our fathers,"—is a well-deserved tribute to the memory of a noble race. They welcomed the explorer Hudson with hospitable entertainment when he first set foot upon our shores; they guarded the infant settlements of the Housatonic from the blood-thirsty hordes of northern invaders, and averted from their friends and neighbors the merciless destruction which fell upon the unhappy dwellers in the Connecticut valley in the French and Indian war. Above all, let it not be forgotten that when the hour came in which our fathers were compelled to take up arms in defence of their liberties, Captain Solomon Wuhannwanwanmeet, the chief of the Stockbridge nation, in the presence of the Commissioners of the United Colonies, pledged the fealty of his tribesmen in the memorable words:—"Wherever you go, we will be by your sides; our bones shall lie with yours. We are determined never to be at peace with the red-coats while they are at variance with you. If we are conquered our lands go with yours; but if you are victorious, we hope you will help us to recover our just rights."[1] Let history tell how on many a well-fought field this brave and generous people redeemed the pledge of their chosen leader.

In 1629 the Council of the West India Company granted important concessions to such as should plant colonies in New

---

1. In April, 1774, the Provincial Congress of Massachusetts sent a message addressed to "Captain Solomon Abhannuanwaumut, chief sachem of the Moheakonnuck Indians" at Stockbridge, apprising them of the probable outbreak of hostilities, and expressing a desire for continued friendly relations with his nation. In reply Captain Solomon visited Boston, and delivered a notable speech, pledging the fealty of his tribe (Ruttenber's Indians of Hudson's River, 209, 270). When the alarm came from Lexington, they took the field and participated in the battle of Bunker Hill. Subsequently Captain Solomon renewed his pledge at the meeting of the council at Albany, in the eloquent language of which an extract is given above.—Col. Hist. N. Y., viii, 636, 637.

Netherland. These persons were authorized to purchase from the Indians such tracts as they might desire, and were legally invested with feudal rights over the lives and persons of their colonists or subjects.[1] Under this privilege Killiaen Van Rensselaer, a wealthy pearl merchant of Amsterdam, purchased in 1630,[2] and at different times thereafter, a tract extending 24 miles along the Hudson river from Beeren island to the mouth of the Mohawk, and 24 miles west and the same distance east from the river, comprising nearly all of the present counties of Albany and Rensselaer, in the state of New York. This grant was known in colonial times as the Manor of Rensselaerwyck.[3] For many years Van Rensselaer's colony was the most prosperous portion of New Amsterdam. An extensive trade in furs was carried on with the natives, the profits of which for the most part found their way into the coffers of the "patroon" or lord of the manor.

The Dutch authorities in New Netherland were from an early day in continual trouble with the people of Connecticut in respect to their boundaries. The pretensions of the Hollanders to the country west of Connecticut river were treated by the New England settlers with ill-concealed contempt. We are quaintly told that the West India Company in 1636, "did cause to be purchased by one Hans Van Der Sluys, a certain place called Kivitshoeck, (Saybrook Point) as their High Mightinesses' arms were affixed to a tree at that place in token of possession; the English not only pulled them down but even carved a buffoon's face in their stead, in gross contempt and disregard of their High Mightinesses; and although satisfaction was repeatedly demanded for this nought has resulted or could be obtained."[4] At last after a lengthy controversy a boundary was fixed by amicable agreement on September 19, 1650, it being provided that all the settlements made by the Connecticut people along the sound as far as, and including the present town of Greenwich, should be given up to the English, and thus peace in that quarter was temporarily restored.[5]

1. Brodhead's Hist. New York, I, 194; O'Callaghan's New Netherland, I, 112.
2. New York Col. Hist., I, 44.
3. See map of Manor of Rensselaerwyck, Doc. Hist. New York, III. facing p. 610.
4. New York Col. Hist. I, 500.
5. Brodhead's Hist. New York, I, 530; Trumbull's Hist. Conn., I, 191; O'Callaghan's New Netherland, II, 151, 152.

The boundary disputes with Massachusetts appear to have commenced in 1659, in which year a grant of land was made by the General Court of the Province of Massachusetts Bay of certain lands opposite Fort Orange. An exploring party was sent out, which spent several weeks in an examination of the shores of the Hudson river, but its commander received very little encouragement from the Dutch Governor Stuyvesant, and he returned without effecting anything of importance.[1] Massachusetts however still persisted in her claim that the upper part of Hudson's river was covered by her patent, though it is difficult to conjecture with what show of reason, inasmuch as the river had beyond question been discovered and colonized by the Dutch, and moreover a proviso in the patent itself, in the most explicit terms, declared it void in respect to any territory in the possession of the Dutch prior to Nov. 3, 1620, the date upon which the charter passed the great seal.[2]

In September, 1664, the colony of New Netherland, the territories of which, with the most utter disregard and violation of all international comity, had been granted by Charles II. to his brother, the Duke of York, was conquered and fell into the hands of the English by the surrender of New Amsterdam. The name of the province was changed to New York, while to Beverwyck was given the name of Albany. In August 1673, the colony was recaptured by the Dutch, but was restored to the English by treaty the following February, and from this time forward the authority of the English in New York was never questioned by any European power.

The reduction of New Amsterdam in 1664 was effected by an expedition under the command of Col. Richard Nicolls, with whom were associated Sir Robert Carr, Col. George Cartwright and Samuel Maverick, as royal commissioners to visit the several colonies in New England. The main object of sending out this commission appears to have been, to secure such alterations in the charters of the several New England colonies as would give to the crown the appointment of their governors and of the commanders of their militia, but in addition

1. Brodhead's Hist. New York, I. 634, 635.
2. Hutchinson's Hist. Massachusetts, I. 130; Brodhead's Hist. New York, I. 65.

to this they were entrusted with various other powers, among which was that of determining the boundaries between the different colonies in disputed cases.[1]   Immediately after the establishment of the Duke's government in New York in 1664, the commissioners accordingly proceeded to execute the somewhat delicate duty of settling the boundary between that province and Connecticut, which after much discussion with the representative of the last mentioned colony, was finally placed at a general distance of about 20 miles east of Hudson's river.[2]   It is necessary to pass over much of interest in connection with this negotiation, and to state what is sufficient for the present purpose, that the line was not wholly surveyed and marked out until as late as 1731.[3]   The northwest corner of Connecticut was then established at a point 20 miles distant from Hudson's river.[4]   This point was marked by a heap of stones, which has ever since been known as "Connecticut old corner" and has formed an important reference point in many subsequent surveys.[5]   In pursuance of the agreement between the provinces, Connecticut ceded to New York, at the same time, a strip along her western border known as the "oblong," the width of which was "One Mile, three-quarters of a Mile, twenty-one rod, and five links," which established the actual northwest corner of Connecticut, that distance further to the eastward.[6]   No change has since been made in the actual position of this corner.

The king's commissioners seem to have been of the opinion that the principle agreed upon for the Connecticut boundary was equally applicable to that of Massachusetts, the "just limits" of which colony say they, "ye Commissioners find to be, Seconnet Brook on ye South West and Merrimack River on ye North East, and two right lines drawn from each of these two

<hr/>

1. The letter of instructions from Charles I. to the commissioners may be found at length in New York Col. Hist., III, 51-54.
2. New York Col. Hist. III, 106; General Entries (Ms.) Office N. Y. Sec'y State, I, 70.
3. New York Sen. Doc. 1857, (No. 105,) p. 160; Conn. Private Laws, II, 1588.   The agreement between the commissioners contains a detailed report of the work of the survey, and may be found in N. Y. Sen. Doc., 1857, No. 105, p. 164.
4. This distance was measured directly upon the surface of the ground, with an allowance of 1½ rods per mile added, to bring it to an approximately horizontal measurement.
5. The geographical position of this corner, according to the latest determination of Prof. H. F. Walling is Lat. 42 deg., 30 min., 50.6 sec., and Long. 73 deg., 31 min., 18.7 sec.
6. New York Sen. Doc., 1857, No. 105, p. 173.

places till it comes to Hudson's River; for that is already planted and given to His Royall Highness."[1]

This semi-official declaration of the extent of the western limits of the Massachusetts Bay was made by the royal commissioners in 1664 or '65. It of course became known to the provincial authorities, who doubtless depended upon it as a justification, if any were needed, of their subsequent action in granting lands to settlers in the Housatonic valley to the eastward of the boundary thus indicated.

The first settlement which was established in the neighborhood of Fort Orange, outside the limits of the patent of Rensselaerwyck, was at Kinderhook, where there appears to have been some few dwellers as early as 1650.[2] The Indian trail eastward from Fort Orange passed through this settlement, and Westenhook or Housatonic, and thence over the mountains to Springfield, and so on to Massachusetts Bay. It was known to the Dutch as "the New England path" and to the dwellers in the Connecticut valley as "the Bay path."

Among the settlers at Kinderhook before 1700 were Conraet Borghghardt[3] and Elias Van Schaak or Scoick, who were extensively engaged in the fur trade with the natives eastward along the New England path. They were both conversant with the native language, and undoubtedly became acquainted with the

---

1. New York Col. Hist., III, 112.

2. The Kinderhook tract was purchased from the Indians, Aug. 14 1698, and patented in part by Gov. Dongan to Jan Hendrick De Bruyn, Dec. 10, 1686. The Kinderhook patent proper was granted by Gov. Nicolls, Mar. 14, 1687.—New York Archives, Book vi. Patents, pp. 154-156.

3. Conraet Borghghardt was born about 1677, and was one of the early inhabitants of Kinderhook. He may have been a native of Holland. He is mentioned as a prominent citizen of K. in 1702, and in 1720, and appears to have lived near the river, north of Kinderhook creek, in what is now Stuyvesant. In 1717 he became involved in a dispute with Van Rensselaer in respect to land titles, and doubtless as a result of this, allied himself with the interests of the New England settlers in the Housatonic valley. Being well acquainted with the Indians and conversant with their language and customs, he was employed by the settling committee in 1724, to negotiate the purchase of the lands forming the southern portion of Berkshire county. He had a large family of sons and daughters, and about 1724, he removed to the Housatonic settlement bringing his family with him. His homestead occupied a site about fifteen rods south of the Sedgwick Institute in Great Barrington, but he owned besides, several hundred acres of the best lands now within Great Barrington and Egremont. He was a man of great intelligence, enterprise, and public spirit, as well as of sturdy integrity, and judging from his autograph, was a man of good education for those times. The maiden name of his wife was Geele Van Wye. Their descendants are still numerous in Southern Berkshire, although the name is now commonly written Burghardt or Burget. Mr. Borghghardt died about 1750, and was undoubtedly buried in the vicinity of others of his family in the south burial ground at Great Barrington. It is to be regretted that no suitably inscribed monument perpetuates the memory of this sturdy patriarch, who may fairly be entitled to be called the founder of the Housatonic colony. For many interesting particulars of his life see Taylor's History of Great Barrington. 107-110.

valley of the Housatonic at a very early period, as it lay at a distance of not more than a day's journey from Kinderhook. In the spring of 1717 Borghghardt and Van Schaak made application to the Governor of New York for a license to purchase 4,000 acres of land comprised in a tract lying southeast of the patent which had been granted to the inhabitants of Kinderhook in 1683, and west of the limits of the Westenhook patent.[1] The land was duly laid out by the government surveyor in the fall of the same year,[2] but was immediately claimed by Henry Van Rensselaer as he alleged by virtue of a prior patent,[3] a claim which led to a controversy the ultimate results of which were far from unimportant.

In order to understand the mutual relations of the different land patents in this region granted prior to 1720, it will be necessary to refer briefly to their histories. In 1682, a tract of land previously purchased from the native owners in behalf of the proprietor or patroon of Rensselaerwyck, was confirmed to Stephen Van Cortland, director of the manor or colony. This tract, known as *Potkook*, was described in the Indian deed as extending along the river from a certain kill north of Claverack, to a kill called *Wayan-kassek*, eastward "half a day's journey" to the "high woodland" *Wawanaquasik*, and northward to the before mentioned kill of Claverack.[4] Wawanaquasik[5] is to this day a well-known landmark, situated between nine and ten miles from the river, "where the Indians have laid several

1.   New York Land Papers, (Ms.) vi, 150.
2.   Ibid. vi, 101, 178, 114.
3.   Ibid. viii, 150.
4.   Holgate's Amer. Genealogy, 98.
5.   Wawanaquasick, "where the heaps of stones lye," has its plural in *waara*; *wa* signifies "good;" *quas* is "stone" or "stones," and *ick* "place." (Ruttenber's Indians of Hudson's River, 378.) This landmark is first mentioned in the deed of confirmation given to Stephen Van Cortland by four Indians, on the 13th of Oct. 1682, for the tract afterwards called the Claverack Manor. (Holgate's Amer. Genealogy, 98.) And again in the patent of Livingston, granted by Governor Dongan, (Doc. Hist. New York, iii, 621.) It now marks an angle in the boundary between the townships of Claverack and Taghkanick, Columbia county, N. Y. It was common among the aborigines to erect these commemorative heaps of stones, it being an immemorial custom among them, for each person passing to add his contribution to the pile. No satisfactory explanation of the origin or reason of the custom has ever been given. The Indians were often questioned as to it, but were invariably reluctant to talk about it. There were many of these monuments in different places, and it is not unlikely that they were intended for boundaries. They have invariably been located alongside a trail or much traveled path, and usually, though not always, near a spring or stream of water. For further information on this subject with accounts of different monuments, see the narrative of Gideon Hawley, Indian missionary, in Doc. Hist. New York, iii, 610; Taylor's Hist. Great Barrington, 43-48; Dwight's Travels, ii, 84.

heaps of stone together by ancient custom used among them."[1]
A north line from this point to Claverack creek would have included some 23,000 acres. Van Rensselaer's agents however,
perhaps by calling in the aid of a long-distance pedestrian of
surpassing ability, extended the "half day's journey" no less
than 24 miles, to the confluence of the Housatonic and Green
rivers, and then claimed to a line extending thence to the source
of Kinderhook creek, in what is now Hancock, embracing not
only the greater part of the present county of Columbia, but a
considerable section of southwestern Berkshire. By means of
this barefaced fraud, some 175,000 acres of land which had
never been purchased from the Indians at all, were included in
the survey and consequently within the limits of the patent
granted by Governor Dongan in 1683.[2] This patent was thereafter known as the Claverack or lower manor, but by the terms
of the grant, the inhabitants were not subject to the feudal
conditions of the upper manor or colony of Rensselaerwyck.[3]
Killiaen Van Rensselaer, to whom the Claverack manor descended by entail, conveyed it in 1704 to his brother Hendrick
from whom it passed to his eldest son John,[4] who ultimately
found it a most vexatious and troublesome inheritance. It appears therefore that the Van Rensselaer patent of 1683 was the
earliest grant embracing any portion of the territory within the
Housatonic valley.

Among the officials at Albany at this period was a shrewd and
enterprising young Scotchman by the name of Robert Livingston,[5] who held the position of town clerk and secretary for In-

1. Ibid.

2. New York Archives (Ms.) lxxvii, 89. A warrant for the survey of this tract for Hendrick Van Rensselaer is in New York Land Papers (Ms.) viii, 91, and the return of the survey, with map, by James Livingston, deputy surveyor, may be found, ibid. viii. 92. This
survey was made in 1721, and the boundaries are given as above.

3. O'Callaghan's New Netherland, ii, 185.

4. John or Johannes Van Rensselaer, b. 1711, d. 1869, was son of Hendrick V. R., and
father-in-law of Maj. Gen. Philip Schuyler. Holgate's Amer. Genealogy, 44.

5. Robert Livingston, first proprietor of the manor, was b. in Ancram, Scotland, in
1654, emigrated to America in 1674, and settled in Albany. He filled numerous public
offices; was Secretary for Indian affairs, Member of the Executive Council, and Speaker
of the Provincial Assembly, Mayor of Albany, etc. A biographical sketch of him says
that "he died about the year 1728, having been with few intermissions, the recipient of
public favor and patronage from his first arrival in America to the close of his career.
He was a man of unquestionable shrewdness, perseverance and of large acquisitiveness.
His main efforts seem to have been directed principally to securing for himself office,
wealth and special privileges, and every opportunity was seized by him to get the government and the legislature to recognize his manor of Livingston." The larger part of
the manor was devised by him to his eldest son Philip.—Doc. Hist. New York, iii, 725-
726, (note).

dian affairs as early as 1675. He performed the duties of this
important office for nearly fifty years, and in that capacity ac-
quired much information in respect to valuable lands still in the
possession of the natives,—information, which as the sequel will
show, he soon managed to turn to excellent account for his own
interest. On November 12, 1680, Governor Andross approved
his petition for leave to purchase land on the east side of
Hudson's river,[1] and on the 12th of July, 1683, he procured a
deed from the Mahican owners of a tract on Roeloff Jansen's
kill adjacent to the river, having a front of about ten miles and
extending eastwardly " to a cripple bush by the Indians called
Mahaskakook."[2] This locality, there is reason to believe, was
about twelve miles east of the river. On November 4, 1683,
Governor Dongan issued a patent for the land thus purchased.[3]
In the spring of 1685 Livingston presented another petition to
Governor Dongan, in which he set forth his disappointment in
respect to the character of the preceding purchase, which "after a
view and Survey thereof proves much Contrare to Expectation,
very Little being fitt to be Improoved, and whereas there is a
Peece of Land Lyeing upon ye Same Kill called by the Indians
Tachkanick behinde Patkook about Two or 300hund acres,
which in time might Proove a Convenient setlement for your
honr humble Petitioner, he therefore humbly Prays That your
honr would be Pleased to grant him a Lycence to Purchase ye
Same of ye native Proprietors, who are willing to dispose
thereof to your honr humble Petitioner," etc. Upon this petition "200 acres of ye said land was granted," and Livingston
accordingly received a deed from the Indians on August 10th,
of the same year, and on August 27th, Governor Dongan confirmed by patent the purchase as described in the Indian deed.[4]
The next year, Livingston again petitioned the governor to
unite his two former purchases under a "patent of confirmation"
constituting the same manor of Livingston and conferring feudal privileges upon the proprietor, which was granted by the
governor, and the patent issued July 23, 1686.[5] The next year

1. Doc. Hist. New York, III, 628.
2. Ibid, III, 612.
3. Ibid, III, 615.
4. Ibid, III, 617.
5. Ibid, III, 622-627.

Livingston purchased from the natives certain additional lands west and south of Copake lake.[1]

The petitions for these patents were artfully worded by Livingston so as to convey the false impression that both the original grants taken together would comprise but a little over 2,500 acres, but the boundaries, apparently by intention, were described by natural objects under their aboriginal names, and actually encompassed a vast tract, containing at least 175,000 acres and embracing fully one-third of the present county of Columbia. The manor, as afterwards surveyed, included a considerable portion of the arable land comprised within the limits of the present town of Mount Washington.[2] There does not appear to be a particle of evidence that Livingston ever purchased the last mentioned land from the Indians, or indeed any considerable portion of the tract which now forms the northeastern section of Copake, although he had caused them to be included within his manorial grant. This was an eminently characteristic piece of sharp practice, which was destined to cause Livingston's descendants no small amount of trouble.

Thus for a consideration of 930 guilders in wampum, equivalent to $375, and some $200 additional in axes, kettles, knives, blankets and other like commodities, Robert Livingston obtained for himself and his successors the perpetual sovereignty over this princely domain, and inasmuch as in the words of his "humble petition," he had "been at Vast Charges and Expence in Purchaseing the said Tracts and Parcells of Land from the native Indians and also in Settling and Improveing the same," he was only required to pay to the crown an annual quit-rent of 28 shillings. But as he afterwards re-conveyed to the crown 6,000 acres in consideration of £400 sterling, he must have received reimbursement for his "Vast Charges and Expence," so that the remaining 169,000 acres, became virtually a free gift from the royal government.[3]

On July 17, 1705, Peter Schuyler, Derrick Wessells and sev-

---

1. Doc. Hist. New York, III, 624.

2. See map of a survey by John Beatty, Dep. surveyor of New York, October 30, 1714, a fac simile of which is in Doc. Hist. New York, III, facing p. 630.

3. This tract now constitutes the town of Germantown and was purchased by the crown for a colony of German Palatines. Many documents relative to this settlement may be found in Doc. Hist. New York, vol. III.

eral other persons holding offices of trust and profit under the New York government, petitioned for a patent for certain tracts of land lying on a creek called *Westenhook*, beginning at an Indian burying place "hard by Kaphack," thence running up northerly on both sides the said creek to a fall or rift of the same called Sasigtonack,[1] and extending into the woods westerly to the bounds of Kinderhook and Patkook, together with another tract of land also lying on Westenhook creek, extending on both sides from Sasigtonack northerly to another rift called Packwake, and thence westerly to the bounds of the Manor of Kinderhook and Rensselaerwyck. This patent is alleged to be based upon purchases made from the natives, some as early as 1685, and others in 1703 and 1704.[2] It is difficult to determine the extent of this grant from the somewhat obscure description given in the patent granted to the petitioners on September 29, 1705, but it is quite certain that its southerly boundary was the stream now called Salmon creek, which joins the Housatonic near Lime Rock station Connecticut. It extended north to the limestone gorge through which the river flows between Glendale and Stockbridge, which can be identified as *Puck-wus-che* or *Packwake*,[3] and included all the territory to a line four miles east of the river north of the present north line of Sheffield. By the conditions expressed in the grant the patentees were required to clear and make improvements upon some portion of the lands granted within six years, and to pay to the crown an annual quit-rent of £7 10s.

It appears therefore that the Westenhook patent, being limited in a westerly direction by the prior patents of Patkook and Kinderhook, did not in fact comprise any very large amount of the territory now in Massachusetts west of the Housatonic river. No evidence has been discovered tending to show that any actual improvements were ever made under the auspices of the patentees, in compliance with the terms of the grant.

The petition of Borghghardt and Van Scoick in 1717, for the purchase of lands south of the Kinderhook patent, appears to

---

1. *Sasigtonac*, signifying "water splashing over rocks." Taylor identifies this as the falls in the upper part of Great Barrington village.—Hist. Great Barrington, 5.
2. New York Land Papers (Mss.). iv, 53: Taylor's Hist. Great Barrington, 2.
3. *Puck-wake*, a term signifying a bend or elbow, in allusion to the change from a westerly to a southerly course which occurs in the river at this point. It is the place where the unfinished grade line of the Lee and Hudson railroad crosses the river a short distance above Glendale.

have given rise to a controversy with Henry Van Rensselaer, the proprietor of the lower manor, which continued for many years.[1] This circumstance renders it highly probable that Borghghardt, who seems to have been a man of unusual intelligence and enterprise, and possessed of an intimate knowledge of the Westenhook region, determined to enter into the negotiations with some of the prominent men in western Massachusetts, with the understanding that he would co-operate with them in extending the settlements under that government into the valley of the Westenhook or Housatonic. Some scheme of this nature must certainly have been under consideration in the General Court of Massachusetts as early as 1719, for on November 19th of that year it was voted that, " Whereas the divisional line and boundary between this province and the province of New York have never been run, marked out and stated ; and new plantations are issuing forth from that government as well as this; ordered that Samuel Thaxter, William Dudley and John Stoddard, Esq., be a committee to join with such as the government of New York shall appoint, to run and settle the divisional line and boundary between said provinces pursuant to their legal grants."[2] A copy of this resolution was duly transmitted to the governor of New York. The action of the General Court may have been prompted by information received from Borghghardt, and it may also have been due to a knowledge of the fact that the western boundary of Connecticut had been agreed upon, and was about to be definitely surveyed and established at a distance of twenty miles east of Hudson's river. It was obviously the policy of Massachusetts to extend her plantations westward to a corresponding distance as soon as possible, and thus establish a prior claim to the territory by virtue of actual occupancy and settlement, a policy which had been consistently and successfully pursued on the part of Connecticut. Two years more elapsed before anything definite was done. In May, 1722, two petitions were presented signed by 176 inhabitants of Hampshire county asking for grants of lands on the Housatonic river,[3] which were favorably responded to, and a resolution passed and approved by the governor on the 30th of

1. New York Land Papers (Mss.). viii, 156; xxiv, 15; xxxiii, 4.
2. Massachusetts Gen. Court Records.
3. Field's Hist. Berkshire Co., 201; Taylor's Hist. Great Barrington, 14.

June, granting to the petitioners two townships, each containing seven miles square, on the Housatonic river, the first adjacent to the divisional line between Massachusetts and Connecticut, which had been run and marked in 1717,[1] and the second immediately adjacent thereto on the north. A committee was appointed to lay out lands, admit settlers, extinguish the Indian title and generally to manage the affairs of the plantations.[2]

On the 25th of April, 1724, the settling committee met Konkapot and nineteen other Indian owners of the territory, at Westfield, Conraet Borghardt acting as interpreter, and a deed was executed by them, conveying with certain reservations a tract extending four miles east of the river, bounding south on the colony line, north on "ye great Mountain known by ye name of *Mau-sku-fee-haunk*,"[3] and westward "on ye Patten or Colony of New York."[4]

A somewhat remarkable fact connected with this deed is, that the Indians warranted the title to be free of all incumbrances, an unusual provision in such instruments, which would seem to indicate that the grantors regarded the prior sales alleged to have been made to the Westenhook patentees as null and void. An examination of the petition for the Westenhook grant suggests, to say the least, the possibility of fraud. It recited that the petitioners had advanced money and goods to the Indian proprietors of certain lands at Westenhook, who had mortgaged the premises to them, and that the Indians being unable to repay the sums thus advanced, the petitioners had "condescended" to make further advances and take deeds of the lands.[5] It has always been a circumstance difficult of explanation, that the wealthy owners of such a valuable tract as Westenhook never appear to have attempted to establish a single settler on it, and so far as is known, never made the slightest attempt to enforce their rights except by bringing suits for trespass against some of the first individuals who claimed under the Massachusetts grant.[6] But if the Indian title was obtained by

1. Conn. Archives, (Mass.) Colonial Boundaries, III; Bowen's Boundary Disputes, 59.
2. Taylor's Hist. Great Barrington, 14.
3. Probably the elevation now known as Rattlesnake Hill, in Stockbridge.
4. Field's Hist. Berkshire County, 201; Taylor's Hist. Great Barrington, 15. A copy of the deed is printed in the appendix of Taylor p. 488, and also in N. E. Gen. and Hist. Reg., viii. 215.
5. Taylor's Hist. Great Barrington, 2.
6. Ibid, 25.

fraud or compulsion, these honorable New York gentlemen knew very well that no man's scalp would be safe, who attempted to settle under it. Conraet Borghghardt must have been conversant with the facts in the case, and everything which we know of the character of that sturdy pioneer forbids us to suppose that he would have been a party to the conveyance at Westfield, if the prior purchase by the Westenhook patentees of a large part of the same territory had been a *bona-fide* transaction.

There are many evidences that the Indians felt deeply aggrieved by the fraud which had been practiced upon them by Van Rensselaer, Livingston, and the Westenhook patentees, of including within their limits large tracts of land which had never been honorably purchased or paid for. Captain Hendrick Aupaumut,[1] who succeeded Captain Konkapot as chief of the Mahican or Stockbridge nation, in an eloquent address to the Governor of New York at the Albany conference in 1754, tells the story of the wrongs of his countrymen in a forcible and effective manner.

" Fathers: We are greatly rejoiced to see you all here. It is by the will of Heaven that we are met here, and we thank you for this opportunity of seeing you together, as it is a long time since we have had such an one.

" Fathers: Who sit present here, we will just give you a short relation of the long friendship which hath subsisted between the white people of this country and us. Our forefathers had a castle on this river. As one of them walked out he saw something on the river, but was at a loss to know what it was.

1. Capt. Hendrick Aupaumut, who was perhaps the ablest and most distinguished individual of his nation, first appeared in history as the speaker in the conference between the Mahicans and the Mohawk embassadors during the war of 1746. Nothing appears to be known of his birth and parentage. His eloquent and able address to the governor of New York, which we reproduce in full, and his stirring and patriotic speech to the commissioners of the Continental Congress at Albany in 1774, shows the spirit in which himself and his people espoused the cause of their friends, the New England colonists. He welcomed the missionaries among his people, impressing upon them a recognition of his worth, even while refusing to unite with the converts. During the French war he served faithfully and returned to his people with honor. After the revolution, in accordance with a suggestion made by Rev. Mr. Kirkland to Gen. Knox, then secretary of war, (April 22, 1791,) he was employed by the government on missions to the western tribes, and conducted important and successful negotiations with them, which unquestionably served to prepare the way for the victory of Tippecanoe. In the war of 1812, Captain Hendrick joined the American army, was favorably noticed, and promoted to an official position. In all his multifarious public duties he never forgot his people, and one of his last acts was to write a history of his nation. In 1829 he removed to Green Bay, Wis., with the remnant of his tribe, where he was soon after gathered to his fathers. The above particulars are mainly from Ruttenber's Indian Tribes of Hudson's River, p. 320-325. See also Jones' Stockbridge Past and Present, and Stone's Life of Brant, ii. 307.

He took it at first for a great fish. He ran into the castle and gave notice to the other Indians. Two of our forefathers went to see what it was, and found it a vessel with men in it. They immediately joined hands with the people in the vessel and became friends. The white people told them they should not come any further up the river at that time, and said to them they would return back whence they came and come again in a year's time. According to their promise they returned back in a year's time, and came as far up the river as where the old fort stood. Our forefathers invited them on shore and said to them, here we will give you a place to make you a town; it shall be from this place to such a stream, and from the river back up to the hill. Our forefathers told them, though they were now a small people, they would in time multiply and fill up the land they had given to them. After they were ashore some time, some other Indians who had not seen them before looked fiercely at them, and our forefathers observing it, and seeing the white people so few in number, lest they should be destroyed, took and sheltered them under their arms. But it turned out that those Indians did not desire to destroy them, but wished also to have the white people for their friends. At this time which we have now spoken of, the white people were small, but we were very numerous and strong. We defended them in that low state, but now the case is altered. You are numerous and strong; we are few and weak; therefore we expect you to act by us in these circumstances as we did by you in those we have just now related. We view you now as a very large tree which has taken deep root in the ground; whose branches are spread very wide. We stand by the body of this tree and we look around to see if there be any who endeavor to hurt it, and if it should so happen that any are powerful enough to destroy it we are ready to fall with it.

" Fathers: You see how early we made friendship with you. we tied each other in a very strong chain. That chain has not yet been broken. We now clean and rub that chain to make it brighter and stronger, and we determine on our part that it shall never be broken, and we hope you will take care that neither you nor any one else shall break it. And we are greatly rejoiced that peace and friendship have so long subsisted between us.

" Fathers: Don't think strange at what we are about to say. We would say something respecting our lands. When the white people purchased from time to time of us, they said they only wanted to purchase the low lands; they told us the hilly land was good for nothing, and that it was full of wood and stones; but now we see people living all about the hills and woods although they have not purchased the lands. When we inquire of the people who live on these lands what right they have to them, they reply to us, that we are not to be regarded, and that these lands belong to the king; but we were the first possessors of them, and when the king has paid us for them, then they may say they are his. Hunting now has grown very scarce, and we are not like to get our living that way. Therefore we hope our fathers will take care that we are paid for our lands that we may live."[1]

The significance of Captain Hendrick's remarks will appear when we come to discuss the controversies which arose in consequence of the wrongful appropriation of the lands referred to by the New York patentees.

Connract Borghghardt seems henceforth to have identified himself wholly with the interests of the New England settlers. In 1725, before the settling committee commenced operations at Housatonic, they employed him to measure the distance between the Hudson and the Housatonic rivers. Owing to various obstacles interposed by the Westenhook patentees, who by this time had discovered what was going on, he had much difficulty in securing a surveyor, but finally procured one from a distant point, who with the assistance of Mr. Borghghardt and his son, ultimately succeeded in measuring the line.[2] This measurement was undoubtedly made along the dividing line between the Livingston manor and the patent of Patkook, and was for the purpose of determining the position of the colonial boundary. Early in 1726, Messrs. Ashley and Pomeroy of the settling committee established the boundary between the two

1. New York Col. Hist., vi, 881; Ruttenber's Indian Tribes of Hudson's River, 321. An interesting biographical sketch of Aupaumut is given in the last named work. See also Jones' Stockbridge Past and Present.
2. Massachusetts Archives, (Mss.) xlvi, 122; Taylor's Hist. Great Barrington. 25.

townships—which it may be noted, corresponded exactly with
that between two of the Westenhook tracts, and made a rough
survey and division of the lower township.[1] The records are
silent as to the proceedings in the first year of the settlement,
but it is certain that some pioneers found their way to the valley as early as 1726, and one—Matthew Noble of Westfield—
in 1725.[2]

The intelligence of this movement stirred up the Westenhook
patentees. They commenced actions of trespass and ejectment
against some of the settlers,[3] and memorialized Governor Burnet of New York, complaining of the encroachments on their
property by the Massachusetts people.[4] A correspondence ensued
between Governor Burnet and Governor Belcher of Massachusetts, in which the former proposed that "no Innovations be
made on the boundaries of the provinces, till they be settled
either by Agreement, or order from Home."[5] This was assented
to on the part of both governments, an order to that effect having been passed on December 28, 1726, by the General Court
of Massachusetts,[6] while a like order was issued about the same
time by the governor and council of New York. It was also
directed that all actions already commenced by the patentees
against the people of Westenhook be suspended until further
orders.[7] Accordingly in May, 1727, the lieutenant governor of
Massachusetts on the part of that colony issued instructions to
the settling committee at Housatonic, prohibiting the further
laying out of lands, or the prosecution of suits against the New
York claimants.[8] This order greatly embarrassed, although it
probably did not altogether arrest the progress of the settlement
for the next six years. The committee quaintly remark: "Ye
settlement at Housatonnuck was for a considerable time much
impeded and hindered ; but afterwards many of ye settlers, by
themselves or others, got upon ye land, and had ye encouragement of ye General Assembly."[9] A new committee was appointed in the summer of 1733, which acting under the instruc-

1. Taylor's Hist. Great Barrington, 17.
2. Ibid, 102.
3. Ibid, 25.
4. New York Land Papers, (Ms.), x, 4 ; Taylor's Hist. Great Barrington, 20.
5. Gov. Burnet's letter, 1726, in Mass. Archives.
6. Massachusetts Gen. Court Records.
7. New York Council Minutes (Ms.), xv, 190.
8. Taylor's Hist. Great Barrington, 21.
9. Records of Housatonic Proprietary (Ms.), 1 ; Taylor's Hist. Great Barrington, 25.

tions of the General Court, given apparently in utter disregard of the agreement which had been made with New York in 1726, proceeded to parcel out the lands, and confirm the title to the proprietors in severalty.[1] During this period nothing whatever had been done on the part of New York, in reference to the establishment of the boundary, although committees had been appointed for that purpose in 1730 and again in 1732, by the General Court of Massachusetts.[2]

It is probable that in thus giving a tacit if not an open approval to the proceedings at Housatonic, the members of the General Court presumed not only upon the fact that the Westenhook patentees could not, or would not, enforce their claims, but that the New York Assembly were in no wise anxious to incur the expense of settling the boundaries, doubtless for the reason that any territories that might be gained from Massachusetts, would inure to the benefit of the crown and not to that of themselves or their constituents.

In 1739 Governor Belcher of Massachusetts wrote to Lieutenant Governor Clarke of New York, that he had for nine years been urging the New York government to take some action in respect to the boundary, and that " if after so many Applications from this Government to that of New York, for an Amicable Adjustment of the Boundaries betwixt them, they will not be persuaded to do what is so reasonable, and to preserve Peace and good Neighborhood; your people must be answerable, if any Inconveniences issue upon this Government's proceeding to settle such Lands as they judge they have a just Right to."[3] Upon the receipt of this communication Lieutenant Governor Clarke wrote to the Lords of Trade asking for instructions from the king, and suggesting that a royal order be obtained forbidding any further surveys and settlements to be made upon the frontier by the New England people.[4] The Lords replied in substance that Massachusetts had acted too hastily in the affair, and that they had directed the governor of

1. Taylor's Hist. Great Barrington, 26.
2. Records Mass. Gen. Court.
3. New York Gen. Assem. Jour., 702.
4. New York Col. Hist. vi. 149.

that province to arrange the controversy amicably, and there the matter rested.[1]

In 1740 the Massachusetts General Court again appointed boundary commissioners, but when its action was laid by the governor of New York before his council, that body expressed the opinion that "as the soil of this province belongs to his Majesty, his Honor cannot grant any power to the commissioner of this province to make any agreements, the commissioner shall enter into conclusive, until the same shall first have received his Majesty's approbation."[2]

From this time no official action seems to have been taken for several years by either government. The settling committee at Housatonic had nevertheless proceeded with their work, and in 1736, under instructions from the General Court, laid out the Indian township, now Stockbridge.[3] Meanwhile the settlers continued to improve their lands undisturbed by the Westenhook patentees.

One of the most prominent of the early inhabitants of Sheffield was David Ingersoll; a man of ability and enterprise, but aggressive, avaricious and mercenary; one of those persons who manifest but little regard for the rights of others, so long as they themselves can contrive to keep without the clutches of the law. As a trader in Springfield and Brookfield, Ingersoll had apparently accumulated some property before his removal to Sheffield. From that time forward he was prominent in the history of the settlement as a most persistent and unscrupulous "land-grabber." In 1739, under a fraudulent title, he seized upon the valuable water-power now occupied by the Berkshire Woolen Company at the north end of Great Barrington village, which had been expressly reserved by the settling committee as the joint property of the two townships for the general benefit of the townsmen, where he erected a saw and grist-mill and iron-works. He obtained for himself the office of clerk of the proprietors of the township, and was commissioned a justice of the peace. These various circumstances afforded Ingersoll un-

1. Ibid, vi. 140.
2. New York Council Minutes (Ms.), xix. 67.
3. Field's Hist. Berkshire Co., 340.

usual scope for his dishonest proclivities, and it may be presumed that he did not fail to improve his opportunities, for we find that in 1749 he was ejected from the clerkship of the proprietary, doubtless for excellent reasons, and was thereafter compelled to seek other fields for the exercise of his peculiar abilities.[1]

Sometime prior to 1743, Philip Livingston,[2] son of the original proprietor of the Livingston manor, erected a blast furnace, forge and foundry at Ancram on Roeliff Jansen's kill.[3] The ore for supplying the works was obtained partly from what is now known as the "old bed" at Salisbury, Connecticut, and partly at other points along the western base of the Taconic mountain farther north, in which region a scattered frontier settlement of ore-diggers, charcoal-burners and farmers soon began to grow up. Some few of these straggling pioneers had found their way into the most remote and secluded parts of the manor, at least two or three families having established themselves in the elevated valley between the eastern and western ridges of the Taconic range, now forming the central portion of the town of Mount Washington. This territory, although embraced within the original chartered limits of the manor, had never been alienated by its aboriginal owners,[4] but the settlers who

1. Taylor's Hist. Great Barrington, 122, 123.

2. Philip Livingston, second proprietor of the manor, eldest son of Robert L. and Alida Schuyler, widow of Rev. N. Van Rensselaer, was b. at Albany, 1686. In 1705, he accompanied his uncle Col. Vetch to Quebec, on a mission from the govt. of Mass. Bay to procure an exchange of prisoners. Served in the Port Royal expedition in 1710: appointed a commissioner of Indian affairs at Albany, 1720; became a member of the council in 1725; was commissioner from New York to meet with other commissioners to concert means for carrying on the war and securing alliance of the Indians, 1746, 1747. He continued in public life until his death in New York in 1749. He m. Catherine, daughter of Philip Van Brugh, mayor of Albany, and had 2 sons and 3 daughters.—(Holgate's Am. Genealogy.) In a report on the History of Iron manufacture in the U. S., (U. S. Census Rep., 1880, Art. Iron and Steel, p. 18,) it is stated that the Ancram works were set up by Philip L., "a signer of the Declaration of Independence," an error arising from the similarity of names. Philip appears to have been a man of a character very similar to that of his father. He was apparently implicated in certain fraudulent purchases of lands from the Mohawks near Canajoharie, and which was the source of much subsequent trouble.—(Stone's Life and Times of Sir William Johnson, ii, 176-184.) On the death of Philip, the portion of the manor east of the Albany post road descended to his son Robert.

3. Doc. Hist. New York, iii, 767.

4. It has been asserted by several writers that the Stockbridge Indians in many instances sold lands twice over to interested parties, in utter disregard of former sales, as for example in Stone's Life and Times of Sir William Johnson, ii, 89; but no evidence whatever is brought forward to sustain this charge, while on the other hand there is much to disprove it. Col. George Croghan, Deputy Supt. of Indian affairs under the crown, in an official communication to the Lords of Trade, says: " it may be thought and said by some, that the Indians are a faithless and ungrateful set of Barbarians, and will not stand to any agreements they make with us; but it is well known that they never claimed any right to a Tract of Country, after they sold it with the consent of their Council, and received any consideration, tho' never so trifling."—(Col. Hist. N. Y., vii, 604.) This view of Indian character is consistent with the opinion held by all who were familiar with them, and had no interest in misrepresenting the facts.

were located upon it were none the less claimed by Robert Livingston to be tenants, and were required to pay him an annual rental for the occupancy of their farms.

In a lovely little valley lying in a secluded nook of the mountains, two miles east of the present village of Hillsdale, there dwelt as early as 1740, a somewhat numerous family by the name of Van Guilder, the various members of which are mentioned in the documents of the time as "Stockbridge Indians," but it is most likely that they were the offspring of a Dutch father and an Indian mother.[1] Other individuals of the same family, and in fact the first of them who appears in history, John Van Guilder, lived two or three miles eastward on the other side of the mountain in the locality still known as Guilder Hollow.[2] The Van Guilders appear to have been somewhat of the vagabond-order, half farmers, half fishermen and hunters, and on their occasional visits to the settlements were apt to fall into temptation, and to consume more rum than was good for them, whereby it happened that they not infrequently fell under the purview of the local magistrates. It was perhaps by some such means as this that Esquire Ingersoll discovered that the Mahican ancestors of the Van Guilders had in fact never parted with their title to the lands on Taconic mountain and in the northeast corner of the manor of Livingston, and that there was also extensive tracts claimed by John Van Rensselaer, comprised mostly within the present towns of Hillsdale, Austerlitz and Canaan, the Indian title to which had never been legally extinguished. He further ascertained that the Indians cherished a deep-seated resentment against the descendants and successors of the patentees who had defrauded them of these lands, a feeling which might easily be made an occasion for open hostility.

Here was an opportunity for a land speculation on a grand scale for those times, and the ex-clerk of the Housatonic proprietary appears to have lost no time in setting the requisite

1. Map of Portion of Livingston Manor (Ms.), Hudson Archives. Eight of this family are named among the grantees in the deed of Mar. 29, 1757, (Springfield Records, I. 11,) which included this tract.
2. Guilder Hollow is in the southwestern part of Egremont and is a mere hamlet inhabited by a few farmers.

machinery in motion to enable him to gratify his ruling passion; that of seizing the possessions and improvements of others under a colorable legal title. Accordingly we find strong evidence, tending to show that a combination—such as the modern school of politicians would call a "deal"—was formed about the year 1751, which included a number of prominent citizens of western Massachusetts, the object of which was to procure deeds of these lands for a small compensation, from the legal representatives of the aboriginal owners, cause the same to be granted in townships by the General Court, to themselves and their associates, and then to colonize them with New England settlers, and extend over them the jurisdiction of Massachusetts Bay. There is sufficient evidence to establish the fact that this combination was pretty well represented among the honorable members of the General Court. It is not altogether gratifying to record the fact that leading citizens of Hampshire county, such as Colonel Oliver Partridge, Brigadier General Joseph Dwight, and Col. John Ashley, if not actively concerned with Ingersoll in the prosecution of this unjustifiable and illegal scheme, at least did not scruple to lend to it every assistance which their official positions in the provincial government and their high standing in the community, enabled them to do.

The first step in the conspiracy was to employ emissaries to incite disaffection among the inhabitants in the eastern portions of the Livingston and Rensselaer manors.[1] This was easily accomplished. These people already chafed under the exactions of their landlords and the continual taunts of their eastern neighbors, who, holding their lands in fee under the "Boston government" regarded them with unconcealed contempt as little better than slaves and vassals of the lords of the manors. These borderers, for the most part rude, ignorant and lawless, yet by no means lacking in personal independence and courage, were allured by promises that in case they would join in the proposed movement to establish the authority of Massachusetts over the disputed territory, they need pay no more rent to their feudal landlords, but that the absolute titles to the farms which they severally occupied would be confirmed to them on the

1. Doc. Hist. New York, III. 774.

payment once for all of a nominal sum to the proprietary.[1] Ingersoll claimed that he was acting under the authority of the
Government of Massachusetts Bay, to which he assured the tenants the lands in question belonged.[2] He urged them to resist
the collection of rents by their landlords, a course which some
of the bolder spirits among them at once undertook to follow,
among others Josiah Loomis and George Robinson, recent emigrants from Connecticut, and Michael Hallenbeck, a tenant of
thirty years standing.[3]

Robert Livingston, Jr., who upon the death of his father
Philip in 1749, had succeeded him as lord of the manor, although apparently not of an especially aggressive disposition,
was nevertheless possessed of sufficient firmness and determination to render him disposed to maintain his rights to the fullest
extent. Under the advice of his attorneys he commenced proceedings in ejectment against Hallenbeck and Loomis, who occupied neighboring farms in the elevated valley on Taconic
mountain.[4]

Not long after this action had been taken Livingston received
a letter to the following effect:—

" March 24, 1752.

"SIR:—In consequence of an order of a Committee of the
General Court of the Province of Massachusetts Bay to lay out
Equivalents in the Province land, I have begun on the East
side of Tackinick Barrick,[5] and laid out a large Farm which
encompasses the Dwellings of Michael Hallenbeck and Josiah
Loomis, and you may depend on it the Province will assert
their rights to said land. I have heard you have sued the one
and threatened the other, which possibly may not turn out to
your advantage. I should have gladly seen you and talked of
the affair with calmness and in a friendly manner, which I hope

1. Doc. Hist. New York. III. 746; Ibid. 807.
2. Ibid. III. 746.
3. Ibid. III. 729, 730.
4. Recent Investigations by H. F. Keith, C. E., of Great Barrington, have identified the clearing occupied by Josiah Loomis at this time, with the farm now or recently owned by John Hughes of Mount Washington. Hallenbeck's location was not improbably adjacent to that of Loomis on the south.
5. "Taconic Barrick" appears to have been a local name for the elevation now called Cedar mountain, and was probably given by reason of its pyramidical outline when viewed from some parts of the Hudson valley, having a fancied resemblance to the "barracks" for storing hay and grain, much used by the Dutch settlers, and by their descendants to this day, consisting of a movable roof of thatch, fitted to slide up and down on four stout posts.

to have an opportunity to do. In the meantime, I am, Sir,
your very humble servant,

OUR PARTRIDGE.[1]

It is scarcely necessary to enlarge upon the utterly illegal and
indefensible character of this proceeding, even though carried
out, as it was, under the apparent sanction of the General Court.
The members from Hampshire county had, it appears, made
representations to that body to the effect that Loomis and Hallenbeck, having unwittingly encroached upon certain ungranted
public lands to the westward of Sheffield, desired that the province would sell them the lands which they occupied,[2] a common
mode of procedure in such cases, and therefore not calculated
to attract particular attention, in the present instance.

A committee, of which Colonel Partridge was chairman, was
accordingly appointed by the General Court to lay out the
lands. There can be no doubt that Partridge and his fellow
delegates from Hampshire county must have been perfectly
well aware that these lands had remained in peaceable and un-
interrupted possession of the Livingston family, under a grant
from the province of New York, for nearly 70 years. In fact
the testimony subsequently taken by this committee showed
that the farm at that time occupied by Michael Hallenbeck had
been cleared and actually occupied since 1692, and that of William Race since 1727. The evidence of the affidavits in the
controversy establishes the fact that the earliest permanent settlements in the present county of Berkshire were made on Taconic mountain at least thirty years before the advent of the
Westfield emigrants, who have hitherto been supposed to be
the pioneer settlers of the region.[3]

Whatever may have been the defects in Livingston's title, it
was clearly a matter over which the Massachusetts government
had no rightful jurisdiction. It could not at this time set up a
color of title even under an Indian deed, for the records show
that the conveyance from the Stockbridge Indians which included Taconic mountain and the lands to the westward was not
made until five years afterward.[4] By the skilful use of ex-parte

1. Ibid, III, 730.
2. New York Archives, (Ms.), lxxviii, 604; Doc. Hist. New York. III, 734.
3. Massachusetts Archives, (Ms.), xlvi, 807.
4. Springfield Records, (Ms.), i, 11.

representations, the conspirators had nevertheless succeeded in clothing themselves with the authority of the General Court, which was all they needed to carry out their schemes. As we have seen, the chairman of the committee did not even have the ordinary courtesy to notify Livingston of its proposed action, but went on and laid out the lands during the winter of 1751-2, taking particular care not to inform him what had been done until about the time of the adjournment of the General Court, doubtless in order that all discussion upon his action might be deferred until the following year.

The somewhat offensive tone of Colonel Partridge's communication probably did not tend to diminish the feelings of resentment with which the lord of the manor regarded this bold intrusion upon his property and privileges. He immediately addressed a communication to the governor of the province of New York rehearsing his grievances at great length, begging that official to order the apprehension and committal of such persons as should disturb him in his possessions under color of authority from Massachusetts Bay, and requesting that "all further proceedings might be stayed in the premises until the true division line be settled between the two colonies."[1]

The Westenhook patentees, after having remained quiet for a quarter of a century, also began to show renewed signs of life. They sent in a petition of like import, in which they referred to the peremptory orders issued by both governments in 1726, prohibiting further settlements in the disputed territory until the division line should be established, and set forth that while they themselves had complied with the injunction, "the inhabitants of Massachusetts Bay not long afterwards had settled in great numbers at Westenhook," and had since continued in possession without disturbance from the patentees. In conclusion the petitioners requested that measures be taken for their relief and for the final settlement of the controversy.[2]

These petitions, together with reports thereupon from the attorney-general and surveyor-general of the province, were in due time referred to the governor and council, and on March 2,

---

1. New York Archives, (Ms.), lxxvii, 30, 40; Doc. Hist. New York, III, 727.
2. New York Archives, (Ms.), lxxvii, 46, 47.

1753, James De Lancey reported in behalf of a committee of the council, setting forth in detail the claims of New York to the territory occupied by Massachusetts west of Connecticut river, both under the Dutch title of discovery and occupation, and under the royal grant to the Duke of York in 1674, and contending that whatever original title Massachusetts might have had to the territory to dispute under the patents of James in 1606 and 1620 had become void by the revocation of her colonial charter in 1684. The report concludes as follows: —"The committee are of opinion, the attempts of the inhabitants of Massachusetts Bay to make encroachments upon any lands granted by Letters Patent under the Great Seal of New York, or upon any lands within the Jurisdiction of this Province, are disrespectful to his Majesty's Authority, tend to the Disturbance of his Subjects of this Province, and may be the Cause of great Mischiefs and Disorders. That the steps taken by the said Inhabitants, even were the Bounds doubtful and unsettled, are intrusions and disrespectful to his Majesty's Authority."[1] A copy of Livingston's petition and of the above report was forwarded to Lieutenant Governor Phips of Massachusetts.

In the meantime David Ingersoll and his associates had not been idle. Under date of November 22, 1752, a petition was forwarded to the General Court of Massachusetts signed by William Bull and 57 others, most of whom resided within the chartered limits of the Livingston manor, for a grant of land described as follows: "Beginning at the Top of the first great Mountain west of Sheffield running northwesterly with the General Course of the Mountain about nine or ten Miles, and thence turning and running West about six Miles, thence running southerly to the North line of Connecticut, out, thence running Easterly to the first mentioned Boundary."[2] In response to this petition, on December 30, 1752, a committee of three, of which General Joseph Dwight was chairman, was appointed to visit the lands petitioned for, make a valuation of the improvements and report all the particulars in relation to

1. New York Council Minutes (Ms.), xxiii, 55; Doc. Hist. New York, III, 755.
2. Massachusetts Archives (Ms.), cxvi, 32.

the condition of the existing settlements. At the request of
General Dwight, Robert Livingston met the committee at upper
Sheffield on the 8th of May, 1753, and was shown a copy of the
settler's petition. He at once told the committee that he himself claimed most of the lands petitioned for, and desired them
not to value or dispose of them. Upon stating to the committee, in answer to a question, that he claimed under the government of New York, he was asked what right that province had
to the lands in question. Livingston replied by reading the report of the committee of the council, already referred to. The
next day the parties repaired to the vicinity of the disputed territory. Livingston pointed out the boundaries of his estate and
invited the members of the committee to accompany him to his
manor-house on Hudson's river and inspect his title-deeds, which
invitation, however, they did not, as it appears, think proper to
accept.[1]

Some inkling of the character of the methods which had been
employed by Ingersoll in securing names to this petition may
be inferred from the replies made by the tenants to their landlord, when asked by him what had induced them to sign the
document. Some of them replied, no doubt truthfully, that
they had not signed it, and could not understand why their
names were subscribed to it, inasmuch as they had never petitioned, as they understood it, for any of Livingston's lands, but
for lands lying eastward of his east bounds.[2]

Upon the arrival of the committee accompanied by Livingston at Taconic mountain, a great number of the settlers were
found assembled. The committee addressed them, advising
them to remain quiet until the division line was settled, and
such of them as were tenants to pay their rents honestly to their
landlords. Livingston, after entering into a mutual agreement
with the committee that all further proceedings should be stayed
pending the settlement of the line, returned to his manor-house.
The members of the committee, although they may have kept
the letter of the agreement, certainly violated its spirit, for
within ten days afterwards, a surveying party from Sheffield,

1. Doc. Hist. New York, III, 739-49.
2. Ibid. III, 745.

acting under their instructions, commenced to lay out the tract
described in Bull's petition, and to cut a tree-fence around it by
way of taking formal possession of the premises.[1]

Shortly before the visit of the committee, it appears that a
New England man named George Robinson, a tenant on the
mountain and one of the signers of the petition, had been arrested and imprisoned on a charge of trespass at the suit of Livingston, by whose orders his house was also burned to the
ground.[2] The General Court, upon learning of this, ordered
General Dwight to bail and defend Robinson, a procedure
which Livingston emphatically protested against, as "an aiding
and abetting of the said Trespass and Encouragement to future
Trespasses of the like kind."[3] On May 31st, Livingston addressed another urgent petition to Governor Clinton, recounting these proceedings and praying for relief. This was in due
course referred to the Massachusetts government, which replied
by a resolution asserting the rights of their province to be
founded upon grants "as ancient as the year 1620," and expressing the opinion "that therefore it can by no means be advisable
for this Government now to suspend the Exercise of their Jurisdiction, but on the contrary it behooves them to go on in settling the Lands and regulating and governing the Inhabitants
according to the right given them by Charter."[4] Upon receipt
of a copy of this resolution the New York Assembly passed an
act appointing six commissioners to investigate the affair, and
to endeavor to procure a settlement of the boundaries with the
neighboring colonies, subject to the approval of the home government.[5]

In July 1753, the disturbances began to assume a serious as-
pect. It seems that Josiah Loomis, although warned off by
Livingston two years before, as already mentioned, had received
verbal permission from him to raise one more summer crop.
Not content with this, Loomis afterward commenced prepara-
tions for putting in still another crop, whereupon Livingston
sent him notice that if he sowed that crop "he might depend

1. Doc. Hist. N. Y., III, 768.
2. Ibid. III, 751.
3. Ibid. III, 748.
4. New York Archives (Ms.), lxxvii, 110.
5. New York Laws (Van Schaack), 313.

upon it he should not reap it." Loomis nevertheless persisted,
and gave out that "Massachusetts Bay would defend him."
The landlord was as good as his word. Early in June he appeared at the head of a body of sixty armed retainers, who
gathered Loomis's crops and carried them away.[1] One act
quickly led to another. Within a few days a sheriff and posse
from Hampshire county, under a warrant issued by one of the
Sheffield magistrates, probably Ingersoll himself, captured and
imprisoned two of Livingston's men, Robert Van Deusen and
his son John, on a charge of trespass preferred by Loomis.[2] Governor Clinton of New York at once issued a proclamation for
the arrest of Loomis and the other persons concerned in the
capture of the Van Deusens, or of any person entering upon or
trying to take possession of lands granted under the seal of the
province, under pretence of authority from Massachusetts Bay.[3]
He also wrote to Lieutenant Governor Phips of Massachusetts,
stating that he himself had no authority to settle the boundary,
urging that the aggressive proceedings of the Massachusetts settlers might be suspended, and enclosing a copy of the proclamation.[4] Governor Shirley, who had succeeded Phips, replied
that he would refer the matter to the General Court. This
body reported on September 11th, professing a " sincere desire
for peace and good order," but setting forth that they had proposed to appoint commissioners for settling the line, in which
New York declined to join ; that they had sent a committee to
view the premises and that it had been mutually agreed on the
spot between Mr. Livingston and the committee that all proceedings should be stopped, but that nevertheless Livingston
" in a very hostile and riotous manner had entered upon part of
said lands in possession of Josiah Loomis," cut down his wheat,
and much more to the same effect.[5]

In the meantime Michael Hallenbeck, one of the posse who
had assisted in the capture of the Van Deusens, was arrested
under the New York governor's proclamation, and committed
to Dutchess county jail, from which he however soon effected

1. Doc. Hist. New York, III, 755, 794.
2. Ibid, III, 791.
3. Ibid, III, 751.
4. Ibid, III, 740.
5. New York Archives (Ms.), lxxviii. 157; Doc. Hist. New York, III, 754.

his escape, and in company with his disaffected neighbor, Josiah Loomis, sought the counsel and protection of Esquire Ingersoll. who it appears took them both with him to Boston. In the latter part of January, 1754, Hallenbeck and Loomis reappeared on Taconic mountain, and exultingly informed the settlers that the General Court at Boston had given them each £10 in reimbursement of their expenses, and that a committee would be sent in March to lay out a township.[1]

This was not done however, so far as the records show, until the succeeding year, and in the meantime matters on the border remained comparatively quiet. The only event of importance was a report presented by a committee of the General Court of Massachusetts, a copy of which was sent to the New York authorities, in which for the first time, the grounds of the claim of Massachusetts to the disputed territories were distinctly formulated. Briefly stated, it was that the charter of 1620 granted all lands westward to the South Sea not actually in the possession of any Christian prince or state; that the new charter of 1691 expressly included all territories comprised within the first grant, that the lands in dispute were not in the possession of the Dutch in 1620, and that therefore they rightfully belonged to Massachusetts.[2]

Much controversy and recrimination was caused about this time on account of the arrest by order of Livingston of one Payne, charged with the destruction of 1,100 trees near Ancram furnace, who was imprisoned for sometime in Albany jail in default of bail to the amount of £1,000, which was subsequently furnished by Colonel Lydius under the direction of the Boston government, and the prisoner set at large.[3]

During the winter of 1754–5, the syndicate of Hampshire land speculators, already referred to, induced the General Court to appoint a committee to lay out three new townships within the territories claimed by New York. Two or three of the disaffected tenants, instigated by Ingersoll, were meanwhile industriously engaged in stirring up the others against their landlord.[4]

1. New York Archives (Ms.), lxxviii, 67; Doc. Hist. New York, III, 757.
2. New York Archives (Ms.), lxxviii, 61.
3. Doc. Hist. New York, III, 707–774; Ibid, 814.
4. Ibid, III, 774.

The disturbed condition of affairs on the border, and the ceaseless complaints arising from the lawless proceedings of "that wicked varlet David Ingersoll" and his "parcel of rascally Banditty," as Livingston not inaptly termed them, at length aroused the New York Assembly to make provision for the necessary expenses attending the settlement of a provisional line. Accordingly, in the spring of 1754, commissioners were again appointed, and furnished with explicit instructions, in which the point was most particularly insisted upon that all lands heretofore granted under the authority of New York should be included within her limits.[1] In July the commissioners reported to the Assembly that they had met the Massachusetts commissioners, but were unable to effect anything, the latter claiming that they had no authority to negotiate for a provisional line, whereupon the council recommended the following as a final proposition on the part of the New York government:—

"That Westenhook river should be the bounds or line between the two governments, from the north Line of Connecticut as far as the place where the North line of the Patent of Westenhook crosses that River,[2] being about eighteen miles, that from that place or point on the said River a line should be run Northerly so as to leave Fort Massachusetts one hundred yards Eastward of such line."[3]

This resolution was transmitted by Lieutenant Governor De Lancey to Governor Shirley of Massachusetts, with a letter strongly urging the acceptance of the proposition, but as usual without result. In the meantime the disaffection had extended into the territories claimed by John Van Rensselaer. In 1748 or '49, one Robert Noble[4] had emigrated from Sheffield, and

---

1. New York Council Minutes (Ms.), xxiii, 177; N. Y. Archives (Ms.), lxxviii, 125, 127.
2. This point was *Packwake.* See note 3, p. 26, (ante.)
3. New York Council Minutes (Ms.), xxiii, 208.
4. Robert Noble.—It is to be regretted that so little can be learned of the career of this brave and enterprising leader. The following facts, which have been collected from different sources, may be of interest. Lieutenant Colonel Arthur Noble was a native of Enniskillen, Ireland, who came to New England in 1720, and settled in Georgetown, York Co., Maine. His brother, Ensign Francis, was one of the early inhabitants of Sheffield, Mass. They both fell in the bloody surprise at Minas, Nova Scotia, June 11, 1747. (See N. E. Hist. and Gen. Reg. ix, 101, 112; Halliburton's Hist. Nova Scotia, ii, 132; Williamson's Hist. Maine, ii, 230.) Robert Noble was a son of Francis, the Sheffield settler. April 8, 1747, he was made lieutenant in the company of foot in Brig. Gen. Waldo's regiment, raised in the Province of Massachusetts Bay for the reduction of Canada, in the garrison of Annapolis, N. S. At the close of the war he returned to Sheffield, set-

settled within the alleged limits of the Claverack manor in the vicinity of the present village of East Hillsdale. He was enterprising, courageous and aggressive, and soon became the acknowledged leader of a band of kindred spirits, who were animated by the common purpose, of making a determined and forcible resistance to the claims of Livingston and Van Rensselaer. From 1749 until 1755, a continual emigration had been going on from Sheffield, Canaan, Conn., and other more distant places to the disputed territory. Some of the pioneers in this movement, or "squatters" to use an expressive modern term, had located on the upper waters of the Green river; a considerable number had established themselves along Punsit creek in the vicinity of the present village of Spencertown, N. Y., and still others had planted themselves in the narrow but fertile valleys in the eastern part of Hillsdale.

On the 8th of August, 1754, the hamlet known as "Dutch Hoosick," situated in the northeast corner of the manor of Rensselaerwyck, was surprised, ravaged and destroyed by a body of hostile Canadian Indians, who threw out detached scouting parties as far south as Stockbridge, at which place the house of a settler was attacked and a man and two children killed.[2] These occurrences created the most intense excitement and alarm. Militia companies were organized for defence in nearly every settlement and town in western Hampshire, and forts were hastily constructed at Pontoosuck and other points. A company was raised on Taconic mountain and the adjacent

---

tled his father's estate, and then established himself, about the year 1749, within the territories claimed by Van Rensselaer. The important part which he took in the anti-rent disturbances for several years thereafter has been fully detailed in the text. In 1763 and 1765 he is called in deeds as of Egremont. He married Lydia ———, who was buried from St. James church in Great Barrington, Sept. 11, 1776. His own death occurred about January, 1770, probably in Egremont. He had three children, Benjamin, who m. May Bates; Francis, m. Lavinia ———, who was bapt. in Gt. Barrington, May 10, 1778, and Betsey, who m. John (?) Burget of Great Barrington. In 1778, the Mass. General Court passed an act proscribing certain persons, loyalists, who had departed from the United States, or joined the enemies thereof, among whom were Benjamin and Francis Noble, then of Pittsfield. Francis settled at St. John, N. B., and was one of the refugees to whom were granted the lands on which that city now stands. Benjamin went to New York, where he was killed before the return of peace.—(Sabine's American Loyalists.) It does not appear that any relationship existed between this family and others of the same name, who were among the pioneers from Westfield, and made the first settlement in Sheffield in 1725-6.

1. Among the early settlers in the vicinity of Spencertown were John Dean, John Williams, Seth and Truman Powell, James Sexton, Ephraim Kidder, and families by the name of Osborn, Lawrence, Spencer and Whitmore.—Hough's Gaz. N. Y., 230.

2. Col. Hist. N. Y., vi. 000; Hoyt's Indian Wars. In this raid 14 houses, 28 barns and 28 barracks of wheat were destroyed. (Statement of Capt. Chapin, then in command of Fort Massachusetts).

parts, of which Michael Hallenbeck was commissioned captain, another in the southeastern portion of Claverack manor, commanded by Robert Noble, and still another among the settlers in Spencertown.[1]

Pending the breaking out of further hostilities with the French and Canadian savages, Noble and Hallenbeck found employment for their forces in open resistance to the New York authorities. In February, 1755, a dispute arose between some of the New England settlers and one Joseph Pixley of Claverack, who was employed by Van Rensselaer to attend a grist-mill; in consequence of which Noble with a party of men suddenly made their appearance at the mill, attacked and partly destroyed it.[2] A constable named Clark Pixley assisted by one John Morris attempted to arrest the invaders, but were overpowered and captured by them, and carried away into Massachusetts.[3] Van Rensselaer, in his capacity as a magistrate, at once issued a warrant and ordered Abraham Yates, high sheriff of the county of Albany, to arrest the rioters. Yates accordingly apprehended one Thomas Whitney, who was prominently concerned in the affair at the Claverack mill, but had scarcely more than done so, when the prisoner was rescued by Noble at the head of fifteen or twenty armed men. The sheriff himself was captured at the same time, put under a strong guard and conveyed a prisoner to Sheffield, where one of the magistrates, doubtless Esquire Ingersoll, held him to bail in the sum of £150 to appear for trial in May following.[4]

As soon as the news of this bold outrage reached the ears of Lieutenant Governor De Lancey, he issued a proclamation for the arrest of Noble and his associates.[5] Colonel John Van Rensselaer, accompanied by Sheriff Yates and a posse of about fifty men gathered from Claverack and Ancram, all well armed, set out to suppress the rebellion, and to endeavor to effect the capture of Noble and his partisans. On April 13th, they surrounded the house of Jonathan Darby on Taconic mountain, which was occupied by an assemblage of anti-renters, and suc-

1. Doc. Hist. New York, III, 775, 776, 781.
2. New York Archives (Ms.), lxxx, 108; lxxxii, 8; lxxxiii, 51.
3. Doc. Hist. New York. III. 776.
4. Ibid, III, 777, 780.
5. Ibid, III 785.

ceeded in capturing Josiah Loomis, who from the beginning had
been one of the most prominent and active of the insurgents.
The next day they attacked Noble's fortified house, but Noble
himself, as it appears, had gone to Sheffield to advise Ingersoll
what was going on. Mrs. Noble, with a spirit worthy of her
husband, made the best defence possible by barricading the
doors. The sheriff's party finally broke in, captured some of
Noble's arms and accoutrements, and shortly departed, not however until they had torn down the neighboring house of another
anti-renter named Nehemiah Hopkins. The next morning at
daybreak the Van Rensselaer expedition proceeded to the house
of William Race or Rees, on Taconic mountain and attempted
to arrest him. A violent altercation ensued, in the course of
which Race was instantly killed by the discharge of a gun in
the hands of Matthew Furlong, one of the sheriff's party. News
of this deplorable affair was at once carried to Sheffield, where
it created the most intense excitement. Coroner William Ingersoll summoned a jury and held an inquest over the body,
who returned a verdict of wilful murder.[2] A proclamation was
immediately issued by Lieutenant Governor Phips of Massachusetts, offering £100 reward for the apprehension of the parties engaged in the homicide.

On the 6th of May, acting under the authority of a warrant
issued by Colonel John Ashley, one of the sheriffs of Hampshire county, supported by an armed posse of over one hundred
men under the command of Robert Noble, made a descent upon
Livingston's iron works at Ancram, and captured the entire
force of workmen, on the charge of being implicated in the
killing of Race. These men were taken on horseback through
Connecticut to Springfield where they were all committed to
jail.[3] Furlong however was not among the number. Upon the
subsequent examination of the prisoners before a magistrate, it
was found that no complicity in the homicide could be proven
against any of them, and they were accordingly sent under
guard to Sheffield, with orders that they be held there as hos-
tages, not to be set at liberty until the New York authorities

1. Loomis remained in confinement until the following August when he was released upon request of the Massachusetts government.
2. Doc. Hist. New York, III, 780, 781.
3. Ibid. III, 791, 792.

should release Loomis and the other insurgents then in confinement at Albany.[1]

This Ancram expedition was clearly an unwarrantable outrage, and one which reflects the utmost discredit upon its organizers, Colonel Ashley and Esquire Ingersoll. In the first place there does not appear to have been any evidence that any of the iron-works' employees were implicated in the killing of Race, and in the second place, Ancram lying directly west of Connecticut could not by any pretense of uncertainty in the boundaries be regarded as within the jurisdiction of Massachusetts Bay. The affair was nothing less than a wanton invasion by an armed force, an actual levying of war against a neighboring province, apparently without a shadow of justification. Moreover, the iron-works were at that time engaged on a contract which Livingston had made to supply carriage-wheels and ammunition for the expedition which was being fitted out by the United Colonies against Crown Point and Niagara, for protection against the French, the common enemy. The furnace was thrown out of blast by the arrest of the workmen, several weeks of precious time were lost, and the success of the colonial expedition actually endangered.[2] But Ingersoll and his associates, like many modern politicians, cared but little for the disastrous results that might ensue to the welfare of the public, so long as they were afforded sufficient opportunity to gratify their personal ambitions and revenges.

After performing the exploit to which we have just referred, Noble's army of invasion was employed as body-guard to a party of surveyors, which under the authority of the General Court previously referred to, commenced on May 16th, to lay out the townships west of Sheffield and Stockbridge, which were afterwards known as Taconic and Nobletown.[3]

Within a few months after this time, the land-jobbers' conspiracy met with an irretrievable reverse in the political and financial downfall of the active and unscrupulous Ingersoll. For some unascertained reason, but in all probability mainly on account of his complicity in the Ancram affair, an order was is-

1. Doc. Hist. New York. III. 798, 801.
2. Ibid, III, 811.
3. Ibid, III, 810.

sued by the General Court in August of that year, removing
him from the offices of justice of the peace and captain of militia, and forever disqualifying him from holding any office of
honor or profit under the government. To complete his dis-
comfiture his mills and other property at North Sheffield was
seized upon execution and sold to satisfy the demands of his
creditors. This was a crushing blow to the crafty Ingersoll,
and one from which he never recovered, for although he sur-
vived for many years, he appears to have passed the remainder
of his life in comparative obscurity.[1]

It seems probable that the feeling of indignation excited by
the Ancram outrage led to a more careful investigation by dis-
interested parties of the real state of affairs, through which
means the General Court of Massachusetts at length began to
realize that its authority had been grossly abused and perverted
by a conscienceless cabal of speculators, for the better furtherance of their private ends. It is not unlikely that personal un-
popularity of Ingersoll, together with the circumstance that he
was unquestionably the instigator of the whole business, may
have enabled his more respectable associates in the General
Court to use him as a scape-goat. At all events, we do not find
the Massachusetts government from this time foward lending
its official sanction to schemes of colonization westward of the
traditional 20 mile line.

Although the anti-renters found themselves thus suddenly
bereft both of the moral and pecuniary support of the Massachusetts government, it is not surprising that they were by no
means disposed to submit peaceably to the authority of New
York. In November, 1756, Livingston attempted to dispossess
a tenant named Henry Brusie, but found the place defended by
one Benjamin Franklin, aided by John Van Guilder, the Indian
patriarch of Guilder Hollow, and one of his sons. A melee
ensued, in which one of Livingston's men named Rypenberger
was shot dead by the elder Van Guilder, but the latter and his
son were nevertheless captured and safely lodged in Albany
jail. The numerous remaining members of the Van Guilder
family with one accord vowed vengeance upon Livingston.

1. Taylor's Hist. Great Barrington, 188.

They set out for Stockbridge, threatening to return at the head of the whole tribe and to assassinate him, and burn his manor-house over his head. The authorities however were quickly apprised of their hostile intentions, and an officer and 25 men were detailed by General Abercrombie to guard the manor-house, while Sir William Johnson, Superintendent of Indian affairs, who happened to be at Albany, dispatched a messenger with a letter to Stockbridge, and by the force of his official influence succeeded in preventing the projected raid.[1]

In February, 1756, Governor Hardy had written to the Lords of Trade recounting the lawless proceedings on the borders, and begging that the home government would take proper measures to compel the inhabitants of Massachusetts to keep within their limits "till his Majesty shall please to determine the line of jurisdiction."[2] After some further official correspondence between the parties concerning the matter, the Lords gave a hearing in London in March, 1757, to the resident agents of the respective provinces, in pursuance of which they made a unanimous representation to the King, to the effect that there was little probability that the dispute would ever be determined by agreement, and recommending his majesty to interpose his authority and settle such a line of partition as should, upon consideration of the actual and ancient possessions of both provinces, "appear to be just and equitable." The Lords expressed the opinion that both charters were "so inexplicit and defective that no exclusive inference can be drawn from them with respect to the extent of territory originally intended to be granted by them," and suggested that a line "drawn northerly from a point on the south boundary line of Massachusetts Bay, twenty miles distant due east from Hudson's river, to another point twenty miles distant from the said river due east on that line which divides the Provinces of New Hampshire and the Massachusetts Bay, would be a just and equitable division."[3] It does not appear however that the king took any action in this matter until 1767, and when he did, he referred the determination of the

1. Col Hist. New York, vii. 206, 207; Stone's Life and Times of Sir Wm. Johnson, II. 80.
2. Col. Hist. New York. vii. 87.
3. Ibid, vii. 273.

boundary to commissioners to be appointed by each province. thus leaving the matter exactly where it was before.[1]

The following spring, May 7, 1757, another anti-rent riot occurred at the house of Jonathan Darby on Taconic mountain, between a New York sheriff's posse and a body of thirty-one armed partizans, including several of the Van Guilders, who had fortified themselves within the house. In this affray James Burton and Casper Ham were killed and a number of others wounded.[2] Governor DeLancey at once issued a proclamation ordering the apprehension of every person concerned in the affair at Darby's, and under the authority of this, several of the participants were arrested, and were kept in close confinement in Albany jail for some two years.[3] This vigorous action of the New York authorities suppressed the insurrection for the time, and matters remained comparatively quiet for a considerable period.

In 1762, Josiah Loomis and one Robert Miller of Duchess county, made another attempt to incite an insurrection among Loomis's old neighbors, but were foiled by the prompt action of the governor of New York, who issued a proclamation against the ring-leaders, and ordered the sheriff to suppress all unlawful and riotous gatherings, at all hazards, and with the whole force at the command of the county.[4]

Four years afterwards the anti-rent disturbances broke out again on the Rensselaer manor with greater violence than ever. Robert Noble, who in the interval had been engaged with his friends David Ingersoll and Josiah Loomis in the more peaceful occupation of establishing a Protestant Episcopal church in North Sheffield (which had now become incorporated as a separate town under the name of Great Barrington,) of which church he had been chosen one of the wardens.[5] put himself at the head of an armed force, and actually defeated a strong posse headed by the sheriff of Albany, who were attempting to dispossess some of the "squatters" on the Van Rensselaer tract. In this affray Cornelius Ten Broeck, one of the posse, and

1. Col. Hist. New York, viii, 889.
2. Doc. Hist. New York, ii, 744; iii, 819; Col. Hist. New York, vii, 279.
3. Doc. Hist. New York, iii, 821, 824.
4. Ibid, iii, 825, 826.
5. Taylor's Hist. Great Barrington, 197.

Thomas Whitney, Noble's lieutenant and right-hand man, were killed, and several on both sides wounded.[1] Whitney was ever after regarded in his own neighborhood as a martyr to the cause of anti-rentism, and an elaborate head-stone was erected over his grave in the little cemetery at North Hillsdale. This renewed outbreak was followed by another proclamation from the governor ordering the arrest of Robert Noble, for whom a reward of £100 was offered.[2] The sheriff with a large posse attacked Noble's fortified house and attempted to arrest him, but both he and his associate Josiah Loomis, although out-numbered and overpowered, effected their escape into the neighboring jurisdiction, and we hear no more of them on the New York side of the line. The rank and file of the rioters, however, were not reduced to subjection until the arrival of a detachment of the Royal Infantry, which had been sent from New York to support the civil authorities.

Pursuant to the royal decree, commissioners were again appointed by the legislatures of both provinces for the purpose of settling the boundary, who met at New Haven on the first of October, 1767. The commissioners of Massachusetts first proposed a line 12 miles east of Hudson's river and parallel to its general course, to which the New York commissioners replied by proposing a similar line 30 miles from the river. The Massachusetts commissioners declined to entertain the last named proposition at all, and proposed instead a line extending due north from "Connecticut old corner," a point "esteemed to be 20 miles from Hudson's river," until it met the north line of their province. New York refused to agree to this proposal, the obvious design of which was to extend the jurisdiction of Massachusetts over all the settlements which had been made without legal authority in the territories west of the Taconic mountains comprised in Nobletown, Spencertown and New Canaan, but expressed a willingness to accept a line 24 miles from the river, in order to save to New York the "rights" of the Rensselaer family. Finally Massachusetts agreed to accept the straight line recommended by the Lords of Trade, having each

1. Doc. Hist. New York, III, 831.
2. Ibid. III, 830.

of its termini 20 miles due east of the river, and stated that they could not consent to "anything more disadvantageous." In reply to this, the New York commissioners, while expressing their willingness to accept a line 20 miles from the river, insisted that its terminal point on the northern boundary of Massachusetts should be found by means of a measurement at right-angles to the general course of the river, which is here considerably to the east of north. After approaching so near to an agreement, the two lines proposed being scarcely a mile apart at their northern extremities and meeting in a common point at the south, neither party would make any further concession and the conference broke up. In February following the General Court of Massachusetts resolved that it would agree to the last proposal made by its commissioners, and further conceded that the distance might be determined in horizontal measure.[1] Thus the matter rested for ten years.

In 1772, the authorities of New York succeeded in arresting the principal members of a gang of counterfeiters which had for sometime infested the debatable territory near the boundary. A number of these were tried, sentenced to death, and executed at Albany, among others one Gill Belcher of Great Barrington, whose workshop tradition affirms to have been in the natural hiding-place east of Great Barrington village, since known as Belcher's cave.[2] The counterfeits were of New York currency. They were manufactured in Great Barrington and Sheffield, by Belcher and one Ethan Lewis, and were passed by confederates at convenient points in the vicinity of the boundary.[3] The arrest of these worthies led to new complications between the two governments, which at least served to emphasize the necessity of establishing a certain and definite line of jurisdiction.

1. The Journal of the proceedings of the commissioners at the New Haven conference may be found in full in New York Gen. Assembly Journal, 11-29.
2. Taylor's Hist. Great Barrington, 218.
3. This organization of counterfeiters appears to have been a very extensive one, and to have caused a great deal of trouble both to the inhabitants and to the authorities, all along the New York frontier from Vermont to Long Island sound. In the New York Archives, (vol. xclx, 49-50,) are preserved a number of petitions for executive clemency, in which many interesting and curious facts are incidentally disclosed. Among these petitioners are Gill Belcher, above referred to, John Smith (of course), John Wall Lovely and Dr. Joseph Bill. It appears that Lovely and one William Hubbard or Hulbert, a son of Obadiah Hubbard of Enfield, Conn., turned state's evidence against their confederates, which led to their arrest and conviction, and in view of his services in this matter, and of his previous good character, Hubbard was pardoned by Gov. Tryon on January 8, 1773. It is probable that most of the others, if not all of them, suffered the penalty of their crimes.

Accordingly in May, 1773 another set of commissioners met at Hartford, at which Tryon and Hutchinson, the royal governors of the respective provinces, were present. A survey which had been made by Mr. Young on the ice the preceeding winter was laid before the joint commission, which showed that the general course of Hudson's river between the respective points of intersection of the north and south lines of the Massachusetts patent, was north 21 deg. 10 min. 30 sec. east. When both parties are desirous to agree, there is usually not much difficulty in arriving at a result, and after a very brief discussion this tedious and discreditable controversy, which had now continued for more than a century, was terminated by the execution of a mutual indenture, that the line should be run from "Connecticut old corner" parallel to the general course of Hudson's river, viz: north 21 deg. 10 min. 30 sec. east, as determined by Mr. Young, till it intersected the northern line of the province, which was precisely the boundary which had been recommended by the king's commissioners ninety-nine years before.[1]

It would seem that when the initial point and direction of the line had been definitely agreed upon, the comparatively simple operation of tracing it upon the ground might have been effected without the further recurrence of captious disputes upon insignificant details, but such was by no means the case. The joint commissioners of the two provinces, accompanied by their respective surveyors and chainmen, met at the "old corner" on the 11th of October following. After running the line on the agreed course about 20 miles northward over the roughest region to be found among the Taconics, a new pretext for contention was found. Major Joseph Hawley, one of the Massachusetts commissioners, happened to discover that the line, which was being run in the usual manner by means of a transit and sight-stakes, would trend a trifle farther east than a line run by the needle, by reason of the progressive increase of the westerly variation as the survey proceeded northward, and he therefore insisted upon altering the course from the beginning. A dispute at once commenced which resulted in the sus-

1. Col. Hist. New York, viii, 871; ibid, III, 230, 231. A copy of the Hartford agreement is in New York Sen. Doc. 1873, No. 108.

pension of the work.[1] Soon after this the troubles immediately preceding the outbreak of the Revolution engrossed public attention to such an extent that nothing further was done in the matter for many years.

On the 25th of September, 1784, another fruitless attempt to run the line was made by a new set of joint commissioners who had been duly appointed by both states. The cause of disagreement this time was in respect to the proper allowance to be made for the change in the declination of the magnetic needle since 1773. After spending some ten days on the spot discussing the subject, and running seven or eight miles of the line, the commissioners were as usual unable to come to any satisfactory agreement, and the work once more suspended.[2]

Finally in 1784, the Massachusetts legislature petitioned Congress for a federal commission. A hearing took place in December of that year, at which both parties were represented,[3] and measures were taken which resulted in the appointment by Congress of Thomas Hutchins,[4] Rev. Dr. John Ewing,[5] and David Rittenhouse,[6] as commissioners.[7] After much legislation and correspondence, the members of the joint commission once more assembled on July 19, 1787, at the "old corner," and after making allowance for the change of variation of the needle since the date of the agreement in 1773, a period of 14 years and 2

1. Report of William Nicoll and Gerard Bancker. New York Archives (Ms.), c, 32; New York Hist. Soc. Coll. 1869, p. 325

2. Report of Gerard Bancker, (Ms.) Clinton Papers, N. Y. State Library, xix, No. 6,530.

3. Journals of Congress, iv, 450.

4. THOMAS HUTCHINS, b, Monmouth, N. J., about 1730 ; entered the military service at an early age, became captain, was an engineer in Gen. Bouquet's expedition against the Shawnees in 1764. Was imprisoned in London in 1779, because of his known devotion to the American cause. Soon afterwards he sailed from France to Charleston, S. C., and joined the army under Greene with the title of "geographer general." He published a number of geographical works which were largely used by Dr. Morse in compiling his American Gazetteer. He d. at Pittsburgh, April 28, 1789.

5. JOHN EWING, D. D., b. Nottingham, Md., June 22, 1732, was pastor of First Presbyterian church of Philadelphia in 1759, and provost of University of Penn., from 1779 until his death in 1802. He was vice president of the Am. Philosophical society, and a man of considerable scientific attainments.

6. DAVID RITTENHOUSE, F. R. S., LL. D., b. April 8, 1732, near Germantown. Penn., taught himself mathematics while a boy on his father's farm, became a distinguished clock-maker, was employed in connection with Mason and Dixon in 1763, in determining the initial point of their survey, which he did with instruments of his own construction. He settled in Philadelphia in 1770, where he manufactured clocks and mathematical instruments; became president of the Am. Philosophical society on the death of Dr. Franklin in 1791 ; was a member of Pennsylvania constitutional convention, state treasurer 1777-89; director of U. S. Mint 1792-5, and was chosen Fellow of the Royal Society in 1795. He was employed in fixing the boundaries of Pennsylvania, New Jersey, New York and other states. D. at Phila., June 20, 1796.—(Barton's Life of Rittenhouse.)

7. Journals of Congress, iv. 607.

months, the line was finally run by transit on a course north 15 deg. 12 min. 9 sec. east (magnetic).   The line was found to pass over an exceedingly rough country, and the commissioners did not reach the northwest corner, near Williamstown, until August 4.   During the survey the instrumental observations were taken by Rittenhouse and Simon De Witt, and the linear measurements were made by Gerard Bancker.   The party consisted of Messrs. Rittenhouse, Ewing, Hutchins, representing the general government, Bancker and De Witt in behalf of New York, and Edwards, Sedgwick and Williams in behalf of Massachusetts, with a number of guides and assistants.   The line when completed was found to measure 50 miles, 41 chains and 79 links in length.[1]   The work was performed with such accuracy, that so far as is known, not the slightest dispute has ever arisen in reference to it during the 98 years which have elapsed since its completion.

The New Haven conference of 1767, while it did not result in an actual agreement, nevertheless came so near it as to render it certain the boundary would ultimately be established at a distance of about 20 miles from Hudson's river, and once that the settlements which had been made by the New England people in Nobletown, Spencertown and New Canaan would fall within the jurisdiction of New York.

In May of that year the proprietors of Spencertown made what was probably their last appeal to the authorities of the old province.   On the 7th of that month, it was "Voted that a memorial be forthwith sent to Boston by the Committee with Noble town and tockonock Requesting the protection of the Government of the massachusetts Bay.   Voted, to join with nobletown in sending a man to see Mr. Ingorsal as an attorney."[2]

So far as appears from the records, Robert Livingston made no further effort to maintain his claim to the lands on Taconic mountain, after the results of the New Haven conference had

1. The journal and field notes of the survey are in Field Book No. 40, in the office of the N. Y. State Engineer and Surveyor, pp. 1-50, and a Ms. map (No. 68 in same office) was copied from the original in the State Department at Washington by Simon De Witt. Another copy is in the Massachusetts Archives, where the writer examined it in 1885.   It is well executed, and exhibits the topography for some little distance on each side of the line.
2. Hist. Columbia County (Art. Spencertown).

indicated the approximate position of the boundary. On March 15th and 29th, 1757, the settlers purchased these lands in two separate parcels from the Stockbridge Indians.[1] These purchases, so far as they were situated to the eastward of the 20-mile line, were confirmed by a grant of the province of Massachusetts Bay in 1774, and lands have since been held under titles derived from the proprietors of this grant. The township was incorporated under its present name of Mount Washington in 1779. It is to be regretted that in their determination to sweep away every vestige of the hated manorial proprietorship, the inhabitants should have gone to the length of replacing the significant and beautiful name of Taconic,[2] by the patriotic but nevertheless inappropriate one of Mount Washington. It is to be hoped that we may yet witness the restoration of the ancient and historical name of the oldest settlement of Berkshire.

In 1768, the "great cause," as it was termed, between the Crown and John Van Rensselaer was tried before Justice Jones at New York. This suit was technically for an intrusion upon the Crown lands, but its real object was to determine the legal extent and limits of the Claverack manor. The verdict of the jury was in favor of Van Rensselaer, but nevertheless for reasons which do not fully appear, in a petition to the governor of New York in 1770, the latter offered to surrender the disputed portion of the Claverack patent on condition of receiving a confirmatory grant of the remainder.[3] This compromise was accordingly effected in 1773, and the eastern portion of the patent

---

1. The first of these tracts corresponds approximately with the present township of Copake, and the Indian deed is in Springfield records (Ms.), i, 144. The second tract is substantially the present town of Mount Washington, and is in Springfield records, i, 11. The conveyance is from Benjamin Kaukeewenoh and others to John Dibble and 10 others, and the consideration is £75.

2. *Taghkan'nuc, Taughkanghulck,* mod. *Taconic* Mts. The name has been said to mean "water enough" and to have been taken from a spring on the west side of Mount Tom in Copake, N. Y., which was a favorite resort of the Indians. (Hough's Gaz. N. Y., 349.) This interpretation is certainly wrong, but of a dozen more probable ones that might be suggested, it cannot be affirmed that any is certainly right. The least objectionable is "forest" or "wilderness," the Delaware *tachanigen* which Zeisberger translates by "woody," "full of woods," but literally "wild land," "forest." A sketch of Shekomeko, (Dutchess county, N. Y.), drawn by a Moravian missionary in 1745, shows in the distance eastward a mountain summit marked "K'takonalschon, the big mountain." (Moravian Memorial, 62,) a name which resolves itself into *ket-takone-waichen,* great woody mountain, i. e. great Taconic mountain. (Trumbull's Indian Names of Conn.) The name is spelled twenty or thirty different ways in the Archives of New York, Massachusetts and Connecticut.

3. New York Land Papers (Ms.) xxix. 55.

was surrendered to the Crown, from which circumstance it was for many years known as the King's district.[1]

In 1771 and 1772, the inhabitants of Nobletown, Spencertown[2] and New Canaan,[3] petitioned the New York government for grants of their respective townships. The sons of Conract Borghghardt also petitioned for a grant of the tract near Kinkerhook, which had been purchased by him from the Indians in 1729,[4] and so also did a number of the Indians themselves, who had served during the French and Indian war, and who represented that the lands they asked for had never been sold by their ancestors.[5]

In 1774, Nathaniel Colver and James Savage were sent to England by the inhabitants of the three townships, to secure a royal grant confirming their titles to the lands on which they were settled, but owing no doubt to the growing disaffection between the colonies and the royal government, they were not successful in their mission.[6] These troubles were not finally terminated until an act of the legislature of the state of New York in 1791, confirmed the title of the settlers to all lands then actually occupied by them. It is a satisfaction to know that these lands at last came into the hands of the persons who had fairly purchased them, and not stolen them from the rightful owners.

After the defeat of the anti-renters in 1766, and the flight of Noble and Loomis into New England, they did not again rally in force—at least under the same pretext,—for a quarter of a century. Many acts of violence occurred within this region during the Revolutionary period, but these perhaps were due in a great measure to the political animosities of the times. In 1791, the disturbances recommenced at Nobletown. An armed mob assembled who threatened and finally assassinated the sheriff of Columbia county while in the performance of his duties. Intense excitement prevailed, but the vigorous measures of the authorities soon quelled the outbreak.[7] The spirit of

1. New York Land Papers (Ms.), xxxii, 188, 137; Ibid, xxxiii, 2. King's district was officially established Mar. 24, 1772.
2. Ibid, xxxii, 114.
3. Ibid, xxxii, 116; xxxiii, 6.
4. Ibid, xxxiii, 4, 5.
5. Ibid, xxxiii, 49, 50.
6. Hough's Gazetteer of N. Y., 291.
7. For a somewhat full account of the anti-rent disturbances in Columbia county, especially subsequent to the Revolution, see History of Columbia County.

anti-rentism, though not dead, was not noticeably manifested for the next fifty years, but in 1839, the disaffected tenants of all the manors combined and perfected an extensive association. They ultimately succeeded in getting the political control of the state into their hands by holding the balance of power between the regular parties, and by well devised legislative measures in virtually dealing a death-blow to the feudal system. This result was but the logical sequence of the policy of dishonesty and greed deliberately adopted by the original lords of the manors. Their unlawful appropriation of unpurchased lands put into the hands of an equally unscrupulous enemy an opportunity for mischief, which he was not slow to use in furtherance of his own ends. The flame of rebellion against the land monopolists, kindled by David Ingersoll in 1752, was not quenched for a century. With now and then an outbreak it smouldered until 1852, when the anti-renters finally triumphed in a test case which had been carried to the Court of Appeals, and to the satisfaction of all good citizens this disturbing element disappeared forever from the political history of the state of New York.

APPENDIX.

TREATY BETWEEN THE MOHAWK AND STOCKBRIDGE INDIANS.

(Connecticut Archives, *Indians*, Book II., p. 225.)

We the Sachems Chiefs and Warriors of the Mohaks assembled this day at Fort Stanwix together with the Indians of Stockbridge in the presence of Sir William Johnson Bart, his Majestie's Superintendent of Indian affairs—do at the desire of the Stockbridge Indians and in consequence of a former promis made them in publick meeting Now declare and make known to all people that we do freely and unanimously yield up and quit any claim we may have had to Lands on the east side of Hudson's River or to any pretensions they the Stockbridge Indians may have along the east bounds of our just and true claims which is bounded by Hudson's River upwards to Fort Edward, thence to Wood Creek and from thence along the same to Lake Champlain and down the same to the mouth of Otter Creek the country to the Westward of which that has not been fairly disposed of by us or our ancestors remaining in us as the rest formerly did, all which the Stockbridge Indians do acknowledge neither are they ever to dispute any sales of Lands formerly made to the eastward of Hudson's River by the Mohawks, at the same time we the Mohacks do acknowledge the tittle of the Scatleock Indians to the Lands east of our Bound. And we the Mohacks and Stockbridge Indians do declare the foregoing Bounds to be Just and true and mutually covenant to abide by the same forever, and we desire that this our agreement may be entered in the superintendent's office that it may be more effectually preserved.

In Testimony whereof we the Chiefs of the Mohacks and Stockbridge Indians have hereunto affixed our marks at Fort Stanwix the 30th Day of September 1768.

ABRAHAM, ⎫
JOHN, ⎬ *Mohack Chiefs.*
HENDRICK, ⎭

JACOB, ⎫
JOHN, ⎬ *Stockbridge Chiefs.*
SOLOMON, ⎭

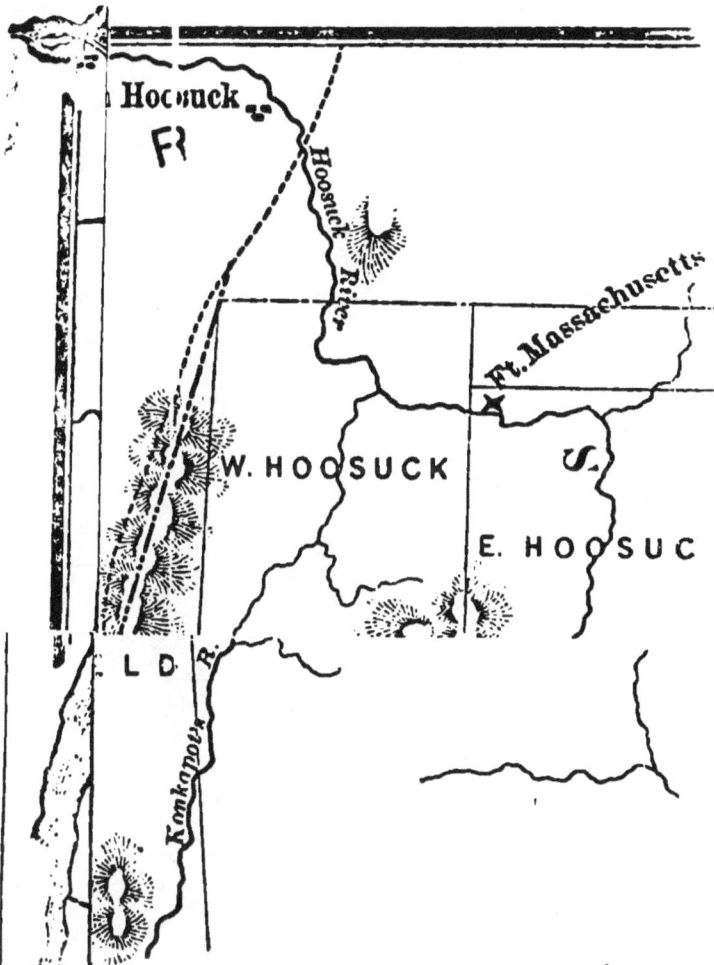

Map of the Boundary Between

MASSACHUSETTS & NEW YORK

SHOWING THE ANCIENT

COLONIAL AND PROVINCIAL GRANTS

AND SETTLEMENTS.

By FRANKLIN LEONARD POPE.

Member of Berkshire Historical and Scientific Society.

Map of the Boundary Between
MASSACHUSETTS & NEW YO
SHOWING THE ANCIENT
COLONIAL AND PROVINCIAL GRAN:
AND SETTLEMENTS
By FRANKLIN LEONARD POPE